GREAT SPIRITS
1000–2000

GREAT SPIRITS
1000–2000

THE FIFTY-TWO CHRISTIANS
WHO MOST INFLUENCED THEIR MILLENNIUM

EDITED BY
SELINA O'GRADY AND JOHN WILKINS

FOREWORD BY
KATHLEEN NORRIS

■ Paulist Press ■ New York ■ Mahwah, N.J.

Illustrations by Rita Corbin.

Copyright © 2002 by The Tablet Publishing Company Ltd. Illustrations and Foreword
© 2002 by Paulist Press, Inc.

Jacket design by Cynthia Dunne ■ *Text design by Joseph E. Petta*

ISBN: 0-8091-0546-2

Published by Paulist Press
997 Macarthur Boulevard
Mahwah, New Jersey 07430 USA

www.paulistpress.com

Printed and bound in the
United States of America

CONTENTS

PREFACE

This book celebrates the second 1,000 years of Christianity through portraits of fifty-two of its most towering spiritual figures. Readers will not necessarily like them all—Iris Murdoch once asked whether any of the saints could be described simply and solely as "good": They were too extreme, she implied. But all of those who are featured are like spiritual stars who have had a profound influence on their age. All of them are also strictly "religious" figures in that they felt bound to the practice of a way of life that held them in total commitment. These are enduring beacons, not meteors that flash into sight and provide a spiritual high and then are gone.

Selection is inevitably idiosyncratic and every reader is bound to feel that some candidates who were omitted should have been given pride of place over some who appear. That element of surprise choice will, we hope, be part of the attraction of this book. We have not attempted to provide an equal balance of men and women, white and black Christians. Representatives of the young churches of Africa and Asia would no doubt be appropriately prominent if this were a volume for the next 1,000 years.

The hardest and most questionable decisions had to be made in the field of the arts, so central to Christian culture through these two millennia. We have included, for example, Fra Angelico but have excluded Michelangelo, whose iconic image of God creating Adam by reaching across the void continues to vibrate today, and Rembrandt, whose paintings are steeped in compassion and an understanding of human striving and failing. And of course that is where our difficulties as editors lay; faced with such a wealth and range of remarkable men and women, it was hard to discard any. At least we can say that the fifty-two men and women selected are indubitably guiding spiritual stars who shine across the centuries—and continue to make demands on us.

We hope that this selection will help to revive an apprecia-tion of the Christian contribution to the world's culture. The total achievement is so powerful that it remains a key to many doors that cannot be unlocked without it. We hope that readers of this book will rediscover the rich tradition of Christian culture and thought and the extraordinary people who created it.

The other great joy of the book was, of course, working with the contributors who have given such vivid accounts of their subjects. The essays were commissioned to appear week by week in the international London-based Catholic journal *The Tablet* throughout the year 2000. Our writers were wonderfully patient with their editors. We set them a truly daunting task: to bring each of these personalities to life while also setting out their achievement for yesterday and today. We hope you will agree they have succeeded.

Selina O'Grady
John Wilkins

FOREWORD

One great strength of the Christian tradition is the way that "great spirits" have always been recognized and celebrated by popular acclaim. It should not surprise us that this is so. Any of us could name persons—parents, grandparents, teachers, pastors, fellow congregants—who have acted as guides and spiritual mentors, people who, like John the Baptist, have inspired us to make our crooked ways straight and turn insurmountable obstacles into the pathways of salvation. Such people alert us to the fact that sainthood begins, not in ourselves, but in the witness of those who by example encourage us to a greater hope and courage. In our gratitude we begin to tell their stories—we are compelled to tell them—and we keep on telling them through the centuries.

In an age when individual experience has been trumpeted as sufficient unto itself, this book reminds us that we need other people to make sense of our lives. And its stories offer quiet assertion that our dependence on what St. Paul termed a "cloud of witnesses" who have gone before us in the faith is not weakness, but an inexhaustible source of strength. It is good to acknowledge that our humble status as storytelling animals is an essential part of our humanity, and recognize that stories of holy people can reveal to us the mysterious ways in which God works through us, often despite ourselves. Why else does it matter that at least one member of St. Thérèse's Carmelite community was not at all impressed with the "sweet little sister who never did anything," or that Karl Barth, arguably the most influential Christian theologian since Thomas Aquinas, began his career as a rural pastor and never bothered to obtain a doctorate in theology.

I find it inspiring that a millennium's worth of "great spirits" should include some who changed the course of church history, and others who are obscure. Many are known to us through their writings, but others wrote nothing at all. I am glad to find so many included here whose theology was expressed not in sermons or scholarship, but in the arts. The Renaissance painter Fra Angelico, for example, or Johann Sebastian Bach. And I am encouraged to find Dante Alighieri, George Herbert, John Bunyan, William Blake, and Fyodor Dostoevsky, who in our age of academic specialization are often relegated to literature courses, given their due as religious thinkers and influences.

Even more importantly, this book provides a useful corrective to the plague of polarization that mars contemporary society, including the Christian church. By extolling not only such icons of liberal Catholicism as Thomas Merton and Dorothy Day but George Fox, founder of the Society of Friends, and William and Catherine Booth, co-founders of the resolutely Protestant Salvation Army, the editors force us to acknowledge that diversity within the Christian church is not a fashionable slogan but a valuable part of our history and tradition. Immersing ourselves in the various lives depicted here, we become convinced that convenient labels such as "liberal" or "conservative" are inherently reductive, and act as impediments to a mature understanding of the faith. Peter Abelard and Francis of Assisi; John of the Cross and Søren Kierkegaard; Mother Teresa and Oscar Romero; Pope John Paul II and the Benedictine monk who became known as Swami Abhishiktananda. We are led to conclude that what we share as Christians is much more important than that which drives us apart, and that this is entirely appropriate in a religion of the way, the truth, and the life.

This book refreshes us with its refusal to offer up plaster saints. But it also makes clear that acknowledging the fact that these "great spirits" were in fact ordinary people, irritable, rash, vain, and all too often prone to failure, does not diminish them, or dilute the divine mystery that illuminates their lives. In the words of a child who was overwhelmed at her first view of stained-glass windows with images from the lives of the saints, they have become for us "people who let the light through." But, as this book continually reminds us, even the greatest spiritual guides and prophets are people with very little sense of their place in church history, no crystal ball to confirm to them that they have chosen the right path. And if we are honest with ourselves, we can admit that this is cause for hope rather than discouragement. Each life documented here teaches us that we are less likely to learn from people who are successful by contemporary standards than from fallible human beings who have been so touched by God's grace that their very faults have been transformed into virtues. The Dominican writer Simon Tugwell once called the human path to holiness a way of imperfection, and I believe that it is the flawed quality of these great lives that gives us hope that our own imperfect selves may contribute to something greater than ourselves, far greater than we know.

Why do we need these stories? Why is it so important to tell them? Dietrich Bonhoeffer once wrote that "Christianity means community through Jesus Christ and in Jesus Christ....God has willed that we should seek and find God's living Word in the witness of a brother or sister....Therefore, we need other Christians who speak God's word to us. We need others again and again when we become uncertain and discouraged, for by ourselves we cannot help ourselves without belying the truth. We need our brother, our sister, as a bearer and proclaimer of the divine word of salvation."

Such terminology might seem accessible only to Christians, but I believe that it holds great meaning for anyone of good will, anyone willing to acknowledge that their way is not the only way. Our tortured world needs people who recognize that being a religious human being means acknowledging our needs for others, including those of other faiths and traditions. I believe that this book contributes to the understanding of how God works in this world, through improbably various means, to sanctify our common humanity. Psalm 84 epitomizes the way that others can teach us that there is something great in us, something so powerful that it can conquer sadness and sorrow. "They are happy, whose strength is in you, / in whose hearts are the roads to Zion. / As they go through the Bitter Valley, / they make it a place of springs..../ They walk with ever-growing strength."

Kathleen Norris

Anselm
(c. 1033–1109)

by Benedicta Ward

Anselm was one of the most attractive of medieval saints as well as one of the greatest thinkers of the world. The fact that he could combine a clear head with a loving heart in the pursuit of union with God is his real claim to sanctity. In 1093, when he was already sixty, he was invited to England as thirty-fifth archbishop of Canterbury, and there he did considerable work for the English church—but he was always more than an archbishop. Canonized and later given the title "doctor of the church," his renown in his own day for incomparable learning was equaled by his reputation for holiness.

Born in 1033 near Mount St. Bernard in Italy, Anselm was a child of the mountains. He told his friends later how as a little boy he had believed that God lived on top of the snow-topped mountains above his home and how in a dream he had climbed up to sit and talk with him. This sense of dynamic ascent and of personal dialogue, climbing always upward toward God in order to enter into his presence as a friend, remained at the center of Anselm's life and thought.

After a turbulent boyhood he left home abruptly upon the death of his mother and wandered in northern France for several years among the excitement of the emerging universities. Finally he became a monk, though not, as he admitted later, for entirely pious reasons. He had become a pupil of Lanfranc of Bec and was working extremely hard when he realized that "if he had become a monk somewhere...he would not have had to put up with anything more severe than what he was now suffering, nor would he lose the reward of his labors." He was professed as a Benedictine monk in the abbey of Bec in 1060; he taught in the school there and was later prior and then abbot.

At Bec he wrote his first brilliant works, including the immensely influential treatise called the *Proslogion*. It contains in its first sections the celebrated "ontological argument" for the existence of God: "God is that than which nothing greater can be thought." It was a simple but revolutionary statement that demonstrates the existence of God as being necessary to reason and is one of the rare parts of medieval philosophical thought still discussed today.

Administrative duties later may have prevented him from producing more, but during his first moments of leisure, when he was an exile from England, he wrote his most important theological work, *Why God Became Man*. In it he rejected the argument of earlier thinkers that because of the Fall the devil held rights over the human race, and presented a new, more hopeful image of a direct confrontation between God and man—in which the death of Christ as both God and Man redeemed all humanity.

Theology was for Anselm "faith seeking understanding," a dynamic and shared pursuit of ultimate truth. He never taught in the schools, but eagerly discussed theology with his friends, wrote for them, prayed for and with them, as well as composing a large number of letters of friendship full of the passion and vigor that characterizes all his works. His thought was linked to his prayer and his influence on the tradition of private meditation was profound.

It was in writing new texts of prayers for private meditation that he was most influential. His eighteen prayers and three meditations were the written form of his own passionate prayers before God and the saints, who were his friends, with whom he still talked as he had as a child in Aosta. "The purpose of the prayers," he wrote, "is to stir up the mind of the reader to the love or fear of God." Instead of recommending the text of the psalms, the staple of earlier ways of meditation, he would give to anyone who asked copies of his own words to God of repentance, self-knowledge, appeal for mercy and thanksgiving. In these prayers he managed the difficult task of combining theological thought with personal devotion without loss to either. "God of truth," he prayed, "I ask that I may receive, that my joy may be full." His search for God was never joyless and it was never static; he

---

stretched his emotions as well as his mind to the utmost in order to come to that "fullness of joy" that is true humanity.

Through his life and writings, Anselm made a more lasting contribution to ways of writing and talking about God than the scholastic theologians who followed him. Though peaceable by inclination, in public life he was no yes-man and held steadily to courses that twice led him into exile for disagreement about the relationship of church and state with two Norman kings, William Rufus and Henry I. His sixteen years in England were hardly peaceful, but when he died in Canterbury during Holy Week in 1109, he had ensured the continuation of the traditions of English Christianity, revitalized into a new age.

□

Sister Benedicta Ward is a reader in the history of Christian spirituality at Oxford University.

Theodosius of the Caves
(c. 1010–1074)

by Simon Franklin

Moderation may not be a quality that comes readily to mind when one thinks of the Russian Orthodox tradition of spirituality. The Holy Fools wallowing in degradation, insult, and excrement; the stern-gazed patriarchs; the principled conservatism of iconography; the impossibly, relentlessly profound liturgical bass; the sinner-saints of Dostoevsky's novels: All can appear polarized, an interplay of fixed extremes. Yet the seams of moderation in Russian spirituality, while not so outwardly visible, run deep into its substrata.

For nearly half a millennium Theodosius of the Caves was arguably the most influential and authoritative figure in Rus Christianity (it is to the ancient land and people of Rus that

European Russians, Ukrainians, and Belorussians trace their common ancestry). Prominent and eminent in the first golden age of East Slav Orthodoxy in the mid–eleventh century (a couple of generations on from the official conversion of his people in the late 980s), Theodosius became the subject of an extensive biography within a decade or so of his death in 1074, by the Kievan monk Nestor. In 1108 he was formally acknowledged as a saint, and his veneration has been constant and secure ever since.

What for? The trouble is that we cannot ask him. Apart from half a dozen brief and dubiously attributed homilies, Theodosius left no corpus of writings. In this he is not unusual. The Rus took what was articulate in their theology from Byzantium and apparently saw little need to supplement it with speculative disquisitions of their own. Their "intellectual silence" sometimes causes problems for modern sensibilities, but the medieval writers were more interested in example than in systematic analysis, and the examples filtered through to the faithful in the repeated cycles of commemoration in the calendar of saints. The native tradition of spirituality was formed and sustained above all by hagiographers, and in this tradition the "real" Theodosius is the Theodosius of Nestor's *Life* and related works.

To start with the practical: Theodosius was the founder of organized monasticism in the Land of the Rus. The Kievan monastery called the Caves emerged in classic fashion. A holy man, Antony, settled in a cave on a hillside outside the town. Followers clustered around him. Theodosius transformed the loose collection of hermits into a fully fledged monastic community modeled on contemporary Constantinopolitan example. The

Caves became by far the most prestigious religious institution of its age, and its influence seeped into all corners of the land. Monks of the Caves were coached to run other monasteries, a fair proportion of bishops were alumni of the Caves, and a significant proportion of early Kievan literature emanates from the Caves. In city after city, cathedrals were built in direct imitation of the main church of the Caves monastery, dedicated to the Dormition of the Mother of God.

The Theodosius of Nestor's *Life*, however, would have been disturbed to see himself presented principally as an institutional empire builder. His personal ascetic credentials were impeccable. When as a youth he set off to join a pilgrimage, his formidable mother caught up with him and "took him by the hair and threw him to the ground and kicked him." Back home she "beat him until her strength gave out...and tied him, and locked him in." And the youth "accepted all this with joy." As a monk he would go out at night, stripped to the waist, and sit until his "entire body was covered by a multitude of flies and gnats, which would eat his flesh and drink his blood." But Theodosius's asceticism was undemonstrative, private. He was suspicious of idiosyncratic display, of ostentatious reclusiveness, and if he led by example it was to reinforce the communal life of work and worship, humility and obedience: carrying the water and the wood, baking bread, spinning wool, singing psalms.

Theodosius's enclosed community also reached out into the wider community. Surplus food was distributed to the poor, and—following Byzantine example—Theodosius established an almshouse. At the other end of the social scale, he was spiritual guide to the prince of Kiev, a kind of quasi-official public conscience. Again, balance was the key. Rebuking a new prince who had usurped the throne, he was careful not to huff and puff himself into banishment or martyrdom, moderating reproach in the interests of reconciliation.

He embodies simple monastic virtues. Lacking universities or higher schools, the Christian culture of early Russia was dominated by monastic culture, and Theodosius of the Caves set the authoritative pattern. His practical achievements guarantee his revered status, while his personal example—though undramatic and perhaps intellectually unexciting—remains a quiet, often underacknowledged but nevertheless constant presence. Every Russian monk (and their numbers have grown astonishingly over the past decade) aspires in some degree to be a likeness of Theodosius.

□

Simon Franklin is a reader in Slavonic studies at the University of Cambridge.

Hildegard of Bingen
(1098–1179)

by Kate Brown

Hildegard of Bingen died at the age of eighty-one, having founded two cloisters; having gone on several long journeys preaching and counseling; having produced hundreds of letters, three great illustrated books of visionary theology, several collections of writings on natural history and medicine, seventy-seven songs for liturgical use in her own and other communities, and the *Ordo Virtutum*, one of the earliest medieval morality plays and the earliest musical play extant. Hers was a formidable personality: charismatic, highly intelligent, kind but rigorous. She heard the music that is the dynamic energy that drives the creation, the music that is the love of God—but also had time to analyze a posset for a headache or chastise the Emperor Frederick

Barbarossa for being childish. She accepted no essential division among mind, soul, and body.

Hildegard was born in 1098, the tenth child of minor German nobility, and was given to the church at the age of eight. She lived enclosed with the anchoress Jutta von Spanheim until she was forty, when, on Jutta's death, she became abbess of the community and built them a new cloister at Bingen on the Rhine.

Her visions were never doubted in her lifetime or afterward—not only her own community but eminent churchmen such as Bernard of Clairvaux and Pope Eugene III accepted them as genuine. She differs radically from other mystics of her own time and later in that she saw her visions with her waking eyes, not in an ecstasy or dream, and was capable of relaying them to a secretary at the same time. She claimed not to rival scholarly theologians, of Paris, for example (Abelard was her contemporary), but in fact clearly read everything and listened with an insatiable curiosity to everyone she could. She had an opinion on everything from the nature of the incarnation to the properties of nettles and found a place for each in the economy of the entire creation. And there is much that is genuinely original, putting together received wisdom and her own experience in an inspired synthesis.

One of the truly original areas she investigated was female physiology and psychology, and she was the first and only Christian writer for centuries not to treat women as essentially imperfect males. Indeed, her entire theological-cosmological system revolved around a radical redemptive concept of the feminine. Drawing on a long tradition, reaching back into the Greek and Judaic past, of understanding divine Wisdom—*Sapientia* or

Sophia—she identified this maternal, nurturing, fertile force as the feminine nature of God. Her complex and dynamic concept of the Virgin and Mother Mary is bound up with this approach—for her, Mary is *Salvatrix* and redeems matter, and women are closer to the image of God than men.

For her, the energy that drives the universe—which she calls *viriditas,* or the greening force—is also the power of the Living Light, which is Love—*caritas.* The expression of this in the creation is music. The original creation was a miracle of equilibrium, of perfect harmony, which the Fall disturbed; the incarnation restores a new harmony—indeed, the Word of God is music itself, and the soul of mankind is symphonic: *symphonialis est anima.*

Here is a woman, talented but also dogged and resourceful, attempting to catch the essence of things by every technique available to her: She describes it in words, she analyzes it, she relates it to the Scriptures, she paints it, she puts it into poetry—and she makes music of it. Judging from the way in which she writes about music right at the end of her life—"Just as the body of Jesus was born of the purity of the Virgin through the operation of the Holy Spirit, so too the singing of praise, the echo of the celestial harmony, is rooted in the Holy Spirit"—of all of these it is music that runs the most deeply and powerfully in her. Here she finds the dynamic expression of the love of God and of his promise to bring mankind back to him, the expression in the body of the green-growing grace of *viriditas.*

◻

Kate Brown is an opera director. In 1998 she wrote and directed A Conversation with Angels, *based on the life and work of Hildegard of Bingen, which was performed in Glasgow and London.*

Bernard of Clairvaux
(c. 1090–1153)

by Christopher Holdsworth

Bernard is usually associated with the monastery of which he was abbot for thirty-eight years. When he died, it was one of the largest communities in western Europe and headed a family of about 170 houses, at least 60 of which were its direct foundations or takeovers of existing communities, stretching from Portugal to Sweden, from Ireland to southern Italy. He had attracted recruits and benefactors in an unprecedented way, turning the Cistercian experiment begun in 1098 into a European movement. Typically, when he entered Cîteaux in 1113, many of his closest relatives and friends accompanied him, a sign of his persuasive powers, which may have induced Stephen Harding, his abbot, to put him in charge of Clairvaux after only two years' monastic experience.

Abbot Bernard struggled to measure up to great monks of the past, to attract others to that same purpose and to make the love that Cistercians took as the binding link of their own community active in the wider society. Until the outbreak of schism in the Western church in 1130, with the double election of Innocent II and Anacletus II, his activity outside Clairvaux centered around northeastern France and through letter-writing to a small outer circle, but afterward it spread wider and wider, making him one of the best-known figures of his world. Why he threw himself into some causes, for example, the attack on Abelard for teaching heresy or the preaching of the Crusade, is hard to understand now; at the time some thought a monk should have avoided them. But as Bernard's ability to move people and even to create peace between former enemies became known, popes and others drew him out into the world so that he was away for months on end. Although Bernard protested that he was useless out of his "nest," once he was, he had considerable effects, though less sometimes than his warmest admirers thought.

Some came to see him as a man of God, combining ascetism with intense personal devotion, and attributed to him those traditional signs of divine power—miracles. Bernard was skeptical about his ability to channel such power, but when preaching the Crusade in Germany he took steps to see that his apparent healings should be listed.

He was one of those who shifted the expression of God's presence in a new direction: It is hard to imagine a Francis without Bernard. His evocation of Bethlehem in his Christmas sermons surely lies behind Francis's creation of a crib at Gubbio in

1223. He made the nativity a very present event, just as he read the story of the bride and bridegroom in the Song of Songs as the story of the present search of the individual for God and his for us. "O Lord, you are so good to the soul who seeks you, what must you be to the one who finds you. More wonderful still, no one can seek you unless he has already found you. You wish to be found that you may be sought for, and sought for to be found" (*On Loving God*, vii, 22).

Anyone, he stressed, could experience this seeking and being found, whose pursuit needed both the affections and the inner imagination to be fed through protracted pondering on the Bible rather than through looking at pictures or sculpture. To encourage others, he revealed more of his own experience than perhaps anyone had done in the West since Augustine or was to do again until Petrarch in the fourteenth century, writing both of his difficulties and of those times when "he had perceived" God's presence *(Sermon on the Song of Songs)*.

Although he wrote mostly for his own monks, some treatises, including two of the most successful, the short *On Loving God* and the longer *On Consideration*, were not for his community, and he never adopted so "monastic" a tone that anyone who was not a monk would feel excluded. Those trained in the schools might find his allusive, digressive rather than orderly and logical manner more puzzling, but even some of them, like John of Salisbury, found his way with the Bible powerful. Now we are beginning to realize that he read it with Cassian and Augustine as well as Origen in mind and had come to feel like a contemporary of people in the Bible, so that he could address the

Virgin, for example, as though what had happened was still in the making, in contrast to Anselm, to whom that seemed more finished. He is often called the "last of the fathers" but could be hailed as a contemporary of the psalmist, or of Paul, or the bride of the Song of Songs. She, indeed, was his model, both in the search for God and also out in the world, where his more aggressive stance imitated her, "...terrible as an army with banners" (Cant 6:4).

□

Christopher Holdsworth is emeritus professor of medieval history at the University of Exeter.

Peter Abelard
(1079–1142)

by David Luscombe

Many of the facts about Peter Abelard's life and work are not encouraging spiritually. His famous affair with Heloise began when she was entrusted to him as a teenager by her uncle Fulbert in Paris for private tuition. They had a child and married secretly. In revenge, Fulbert had Abelard castrated. The couple separated, Heloise to enter the convent of Argenteuil, where she unwillingly became a nun, Abelard to become a restless monk at the royal abbey of St. Denis and later abbot of St. Gildas. In 1121 his teachings were severely censured at a legatine council held in Soissons; in 1140, following a fierce campaign led by Bernard of Clairvaux, he was again condemned, by Pope Innocent II.

Abelard had an exceptional ability to provoke conflicting opinions about his work and himself. In his early life, when he shone as a teacher of logic, he was a braggart and a scoffer, but he underwent a genuine conversion as he grew older. When Heloise first obtained a copy of his autobiography, she angrily accused him of having messed up her life. All she ever wanted was him. In reply Abelard just urged her to pray.

After he had entered St. Denis as a monk, he devoted himself more intensely to the study of theology. In part he did so in the belief that the application of the tools of logic to theology would clear up misunderstandings. It was this aspect of Abelard's teaching that attracted the greatest criticism, but it should not be exaggerated. He did also promote the primacy of intention over deed in the moral sphere, the importance of Christ's life and death considered as an example, the modalities by which the divine persons communicate themselves to creatures, and the extent to which philosophers in antiquity had come near to Christian faith. He often turned to Augustine of Hippo for support with the latter, and some at least of the criticism heaped upon Abelard arose from what his students said that he had said as distinct from what we find in his surviving works after careful editing. But certainly the breakdown of Abelard's career, first in the schools and then as monk and as abbot, impelled him to search for new bearings, and it is this search that allows us to discover a still neglected spiritual genius.

In 1129, the property of Heloise's community in Argenteuil was reclaimed by (of all places) the abbey of St. Denis. Abelard had some land in the diocese of Troyes in eastern France. He was then abbot of St. Gildas in Brittany, and extremely unhappy. He had previously started an experimental hermitage at Quincey. This too ended in tears, but the idea behind it is key to understanding the man. Abelard had come to believe that true philosophy—literally, love of wisdom—consists of prayer and study practiced in a communal hermitage. He admired models such as Elijah, John the Baptist, St. Anthony of Egypt, and St. Jerome, and he had words of scorn for conventional monasticism. He had called his foundation the oratory of the Paraclete—the Consoler—and when he heard of Heloise's plight he offered the property to her and to those of her sisters who wished to move there. Moreover, he saw himself, once he could get away from St. Gildas, as their superior.

The collected correspondence between himself and Heloise constitutes part of his guidance. The autobiography records the fall that follows pride, and the letters from Heloise, which begin so bitterly, change to requests for information and practical advice. In the most seldom read parts of the collection, Abelard writes movingly of the role of women in the New Testament and eruditely, if eccentrically, on such matters as clothing, silence, food, drink, the office, and so on. This is, however, only a small part of the contribution he made to refounding the Paraclete as a nunnery. He also provided it with a book of sermons, a set of solutions to queries concerning Scripture presented by the nuns, a commentary on Genesis, 133 hymns written and set to music by himself, antiphons, sequences, responses, collects, a lectionary, and a program of study. The latter took its inspiration from Jerome, who likewise had found a role as a guide for religious women, and it reflects Abelard's preoccupation with the importance of prayer along with study as an aid to understanding, and also with poverty and simplicity as the means to detachment from this world. Like Jerome the translator, if less convincingly, he emphasized the need to study the Scriptures in their original languages.

For centuries, Abelard has been regarded as a brilliant logician and a heretical theologian. During the twentieth century a better understanding of his aims as a theologian has been gained. Nowadays it is also possible to see his monastic theology in a positive light. For all his mistakes and limitations, he may now take his place among the pioneers of the monastic reformation of the twelfth century.

◻

David Luscombe is Leverhulme Personal Research Professor of Medieval History at the University of Sheffield.

Francis of Assisi
(1181/82–1226)

by Frances Teresa

One of the surprising things about Francis of Assisi is that almost everyone has heard of him. However, they may not know that he was born about 1181, had been a rich playboy in Assisi, began a long and difficult conversion while a prisoner of war in Perugia, and that his pursuit of the Gospel led to the Franciscan Order. They may not know his anguish, though they often know his joy. They know that he was on the side of the poor and the marginalized, a lover of God and all creation, that he was—and still is—everybody's personal friend and support. They probably do not know that he received the stigmata, nor what that means—but in the truest sense, do any of us? They have certainly grasped the essentials.

Francis's aim was to become as much like Christ as possible. God had made him "to the image of his beloved son according to the body, and to his likeness according to the spirit." He was haunted by the thought that the Word became flesh. This was why he pursued Lady Poverty through a ruthless self-stripping, seeking a total inner and (at the moment of death, outer) nakedness as the truth of himself before God.

We cannot tell whether we see Francis as his contemporaries did. Many thought him quite mad, while others he led to profound conversion. The early Franciscan movement was filled with charismatic and eccentric characters (qualities that have endured in the Order). Francis welcomed everyone who came as a brother sent by God, and in no time at all there were five hundred of them and he had an order full of problems.

In many stories, we see him struggling to live a simple gospel life while thinking about rules and organization—not his forte. Many had joined without knowing him personally and did not agree with him or one another. The result was conflict, argument, and pain. Francis lived, as near as he could, according to God's value system, filled with the generous folly of the cross. Some of the others were tempted to think in terms of clerics, privilege, and a career in the church. Francis never forgot the one who had nowhere to lay his head.

We both see Francis accurately, I suspect, and completely fail to understand him. We are drawn by his intimacy with Christ, his gentleness with the vulnerable, his rapport with animals, and what his biographer calls his "restoration to original innocence." We would like to tame wolves, like those of Gubbio that terrorized the town, and those within ourselves as well. When we read the early stories, we are deceived into thinking it was all fun (and at first it probably was). We are disarmed by his ready dismay at himself—the stories are legion—but think of the time he sent the young, aristocratic Rufino to preach naked in the cathedral of Assisi, and of Francis's quick repentance, going naked into the town to join him. Behind walked his faithful, understanding friend, secretary, confessor, and confidant, Brother Leo, carrying two habits in readiness.

So what was young Clare, Rufino's cousin, thinking when she fled at night to join Francis and his band? No wonder her family was appalled. She compounded this by selling her dowry-land and some of her sister's, giving the proceeds to the poor, promising obedience to this unauthorized, unordained ragamuffin and then working (like Francis) as a servant in the nearby Benedictine monastery—all scandalous but irrevocable steps in thirteenth-century Europe. She was the first to fully share his vision, and in the long years after his death she remained a touchstone of authenticity for the early brethren, so that Leo and the others remained close to her and the first Poor Clares and were present at her deathbed in 1253. How young they were when it all began! For them, Francis was not the fool but the wise man who had sold all he possessed and not only gained the field but the treasure in it.

We cannot begin to plumb the depths of Francis's depression and despair at the conflicts within his order. We find them embarrassing, unsuited to our image of this joyous saint. Nor do we understand that experience on La Verna, from which, two years before his death, he emerged with Christ's own wounds in his hands, feet, and side. Asking to share Christ's love and Christ's pain, he entered into deep and terrible darkness. Eventually, this broke into the joy of his "Canticle of All Creation": "Be praised my Lord, for our Brother Sir Sun, our Sisters Moon, Stars, Water, Brother Wind and all creation." It was the first salvo of Italian poetry and the culminating exultation of a life burnt up with love for God. We cannot understand how such glory, pain, and greatness could exist in such a little, poor man, one so low that nobody is lower, so simple that we understand his every word.

□

Sister Frances Teresa belongs to the Poor Clare community in Arundel, West Sussex, in England.

Dante Alighieri
(1265–1321)

by Eamon Duffy

Dante Alighieri was born in Florence in 1265 and died, exiled by a rival city faction, in Ravenna in 1321. He lived through some of the stormiest events in the history of Italy, including the brief reign and then abdication of the saintly hermit Pope Celestine V. It was Celestine's successor, the worldly Boniface VIII, who proclaimed the first Holy Year of Jubilee in 1300.

Dante was a man of intense ideals and a stern and unforgiving critic of those who did not live up to them. Celestine V's election promised spiritual transformation for a corrupt church: Dante was appalled by his abdication and put him in the first circle of hell for this "great refusal." But Dante loathed even more Boniface VIII, who decreed in the Bull *Unam Sanctam* that "every human creature must be subject to the Roman pontiff." Dante sank him head-first in a molten furnace, one of the gallery of damned popes in the eighth circle. Dante revered the papacy but recoiled from its prostitution by the popes of his time: He tells us sardonically that the traffic arrangements in hell resembled those he saw for the crowds in Rome during the 1300 Jubilee. He was one of many who prayed for a messianic emperor who would pacify Italy and Europe, and give the church holy priests.

Dante's fictional journey through hell, purgatory, and heaven, the *Divine Comedy,* is one of the greatest poems in all of literature, ranking alongside Homer and Shakespeare. It is also the most profound expression of Christian hope outside the New Testament. Moralizing accounts of other-world journeys were common enough in the Middle Ages, but Dante's was unique in the grandeur and wholeness of its vision of good and evil and its majestic account of human destiny. Set in Holy Week and Easter of the Jubilee Year 1300, the poem's visionary journey becomes the fictional Dante's spiritual education.

It opens with the middle-aged poet morally adrift, "in the midst of the journey of our life...astray in a dark wood, where the straight path was lost." As it unfolds, he is harrowed and reduced to penitence by encountering ever deeper pits of human vileness, healed and educated by climbing the mountain of purgatory, shedding the deadly sins as he moves upward, and finally ascends through the circles of heaven, where he moves beyond words to a glimpsed vision of the Trinity itself, "the Love that moves the sun and the other stars."

Love dominates the poem: Over the gates of Hell itself is written, "The primal Love made me," for the damned are those who have turned their backs on love. Dante, steeped in the philosophy of Aristotle, understood damnation not as punishment imposed for breaking the commandments but as the loss of true humanity that follows inevitably when we reject the virtues for which we were created. For Dante as for St. Thomas, the grace of the Gospel perfects but does not supersede human culture and natural virtue. Hence his guide through hell and purgatory is a pagan, the poet Virgil, Dante's "dearest master," excluded forever from the beatific vision by his lack of faith and baptism but able to lead Dante to the very threshold of paradise. He is replaced by Beatrice, the childhood sweetheart who became for Dante the symbol of the demanding presence of God's grace and truth in his own life. Among other things, Dante's poem is a meditation on the meaning of secular culture, rendered tragic by his sense of the insufficiency of even the noblest virtue without grace.

The *Commedia* was unique in theological as well as literary terms. There was no precedent for Dante's purgatory, not a torture-house, but a place of hope and growth, in which therapeutic suffering is eagerly embraced by "fortunate spirits" cooperating in their liberation from the chains that their sins have forged, *"solvendo il nodo"* (dissolving the knot). If the gruesome *Inferno* is more famous, *Purgatorio* is the most touching and accessible section of the poem, its tone struck in the very opening scene as the pilgrims emerge from hell on to the shore, by the first trembling light of dawn on Easter Day. Gently, Virgil washes the tears of grief and horror from the face of the traumatized Dante with handfuls of soft young rushes, which renew themselves as they are plucked: There is no tenderer moment in the whole of poetry.

The *Commedia* is one of the defining sources of Western culture, evoking unforgettable images from artists like Blake and Doré, fertilizing modern poetic masterpieces like Eliot's *Wasteland* and *Four Quartets* or Seamus Heaney's *Station Island*. It is also a great act of spiritual creativity, a majestic and passionate vision that has lost none of its power to challenge, inspire, and force us to our knees.

❑

Eamon Duffy is a reader in church history at the University of Cambridge.

Meister Eckhart
(c. 1260–c. 1328)

by Denys Turner

The influence of Meister Eckhart is probably greater today than at any time since his death. Here is a Christian pastor who in the area of academic theology challenges us from the standpoint of practical piety, and vice versa. For this intensely intellectual Dominican preached sermons to unlettered women in the fourteenth-century Rhineland that fox the best academic minds today with disturbing and technically abstruse paradox. But he also composed academic treatises as a university professor of theology that offer a spiritual challenge still capable of speaking with immediacy and directness across the centuries since his death.

We possess only enough evidence of external events in his life to piece together a bare outline, and evidence of an inner life only from his writings. His vocation as a Dominican led to a varied mix of academic, administrative, and pastoral responsibilities. Twice master of theology at the University of Paris, he was not unusual in passing between academic work and wider responsibilities in the church, for medieval university professors were rarely permanently tenured in the modern fashion. And so he also served at different periods as Dominican prior and provincial and, in the final ten or twelve years of his life, he was appointed to pastoral responsibility for the numerous communities of women, particularly those known as Beguines, which flourished in the Rhineland in the early fourteenth century.

In two ways, this last pastoral responsibility was decisive. For his thought, because it is from this period of his activity that we have many of the writings for which today he is best known, the so-called German Sermons, some of them preached to these congregations of women in Strasbourg and Cologne. And for his life, because it is probably on account of his association with the Beguines that, as an old man, he fell afoul of the archbishop of Cologne, Henry of Virneberg, whose hounding of the Beguine movement had been relentless for over twenty years.

Arraigned in 1326 to the archiepiscopal court at Cologne on charges of heresy, Eckhart appealed to Pope John XXII at Avignon. He lived long enough to present his defense to the investigating commission but died, probably in 1328, a year before the publication of the papal bull *In agro dominico*, in which some twenty-eight propositions, taken mainly from his German Sermons, were declared to be variously "heretical" or "dangerous" or "ill-sounding." We cannot know, therefore, what Eckhart's response would have been to the bull, though he had protested to the tribunal that they were considering propositions taken out of that context in which their meaning was plainly orthodox. It is notable that nearly all the condemned propositions are derived from his vernacular preaching, where we can suppose a quite different rhetorical purpose from that of the careful, formulaic precision of the Latin-speaking academic theologian.

And as a preacher, Eckhart sets out to jolt the mind as a spiritual stratagem. What matters to Eckhart when he preaches is less what his words say, formally speaking, than what the act of saying them does to the minds and hearts of his congregations: In common with many a medieval theologian, Eckhart thought of the language of faith as inherently "sacramental," for it does what it says. But what seems so dauntingly strange to us, as we read those short homilies, is less that Eckhart spectacularly refuses to patronize his audience intellectually than that he seeks out a route direct to the heart through the mind. Modern readers who persevere long enough to understand what he is saying invariably find themselves deeply moved by his words. When he asks his hearers to "take leave of God for the sake of God" and thereby to "sink into the abyss of the divine nothingness," Eckhart is preaching directly to that "ground" of ourselves—our "nothingness"—which, he says, is God.

Eckhart never supposed that good preaching was itself a form of holiness. Yet he was a Dominican in every fiber of his being and it was certainly in order to preach that he sought holiness, and it was in his preaching that his holiness was chiefly embodied. In everything he loved God with his mind; for him, "mind" was simply a passion for God. And he speaks to us at least as paradoxically as he did to his contemporaries because we know perhaps even less about such things than they did.

□

Denys Turner is the Norris-Hulse Professor of Divinity at the University of Cambridge.

Dominic
(c. 1170–1221)

by Richard Finn

The Franciscans in the thirteenth century were resolved to present detailed narratives of their founder's history in words or painting; the Dominicans were not. They did not see Dominic as a unique model for imitation by Christians in all walks of life. His importance for them lay, above all, in his creation of an international religious order dedicated to preaching and its attendant work of reconciling penitents to God.

This Spaniard, born around 1170 in the small town of Caleruega, who started a clerical career as a cathedral canon and priest at Osma, became after 1203 deeply committed to the task of preaching the Catholic faith in the Languedoc in southern France, where it was challenged by the Cathars, or Albigensians.

They were radical dualists: For them the visible world was the work of the devil, whom they presented almost as a rival god. Theirs was a world where women turned into men to enter heaven and the unborn child was spoken of as a demon. Salvation meant escape from matter. Against this the Dominicans defended the truth of the incarnation, the restoration by grace of our good though damaged humanity by the holy humanity of Christ.

What characterized Dominic's approach to this defense was the realization that it required sustained debate, which in turn required lengthy theological study by the preacher and then contact with people in far different circumstances than had formerly prevailed: It was not enough to write a treatise in some distant monastery or to turn up somewhere, preach before the crowd, and go. You had to engage with what others thought and said. Hence the famous story that Dominic spent the whole night in a tavern drinking as he argued with a heretic. A readiness to communicate the faith through debate was more important than preserving traditional appearances of clerical decorum. Yet this contact would prove fruitful only if one's arguments were matched by a certain lifestyle, the mendicant poverty that Cathars and Catholics alike could see as an authentic expression of the apostolic life, faithful to the instructions Jesus had given to the Twelve. Preachers should be beggars.

Until 1215 Dominic's work, in collaboration with Bishop Fulk of Toulouse and a small group of like-minded brethren, is limited to the Languedoc. Thereafter his horizons alter. He swiftly emerges as the founder of an international order, dispersing the small group at Toulouse on the feast of the assumption in

1217 to found houses in Spain and in Paris, Europe's most important center of advanced theological study. Further foundations would soon follow in Rome and Bologna, the second most important university city in Europe, while a band of friars would reach Oxford and its university in 1221. In this sudden development we should almost certainly see the approving hand of Pope Innocent III. Dominic had traveled to Rome in 1215 to win his approval for the Toulouse community.

Pope Innocent may well have been the inspiration behind the larger vision, but Dominic then worked over the next few years to win the support of his successor, Pope Honorius III. Dominic's orbit then shifted from the Languedoc to Italy, where he made frequent visits to the papal court. In 1216 Honorius confirmed the Dominicans' adoption of St. Augustine's Rule. What emerged was a religious order located in all the major university centers of Europe, from which trained recruits could be sent out to preach the orthodoxy and church reforms determined by the Fourth Lateran Council of 1215, with emphasis on the sacraments, the need for regular confession, and the doctrine of transubstantiation. And these friars, unlike monks who had taken a vow of stability to a single abbey or priory, could be moved around and sent where they were most needed.

A story retold by Humbert of Romans, a later master of the Dominican order (1254–1263), suggests the impact made by the friars in medieval society. An Italian anchoress, who saw her spiritual progress and safety as protected by the strict confines of her cell, had been waiting with excitement for her first encounter with these traveling preachers. But when she opened the window and saw how good-looking the young Dominicans were, the shocked anchoress shut the window in their faces. It took a vision of Our Lady to convince her that these new religious could survive such a mission with their virtue intact.

The genius of the saint was to create a structure fit for the purpose, with its insistence on prolonged study of philosophy and theology, its balance of active and contemplative elements, and a legislative and constitutional structure flexible enough to meet the changing circumstances of the mission. Here, too, Dominic seems to have proceeded by way of debate. He allowed others their say in the assemblies or chapters that sorted out how the first brethren were to live and work. The trust he displayed in his brethren gave them the confidence to continue with seemingly no great crisis after his death on 6 August 1221.

□

Richard Finn, a Dominican friar, is vice-regent of studies at Blackfriars, Oxford.

Thomas Aquinas
(c. 1225–1274)

by Herbert McCabe

Thomas Aquinas is generally regarded as the greatest theologian of the Christian church and among the greatest philosophers of the West, yet he can be seen as a kind of atheist and a kind of materialist. An atheist because, like the Ten Commandments, he begins by outlawing any worship of the gods; a materialist because he rejects the dualism that goes back at least to Plato and has powerfully influenced philosophers—the idea that what I consist of is a mechanism called a body linked in some way with a "self" or "soul" contrasting with the body and making me personally Me. The greatest exponent of this view in early modern times was René Descartes at the beginning of the seventeenth century. In the last century Ludwig Wittgenstein began the anti-Cartesian revolution and brought us back in some ways to the originality of Aquinas's thinking.

One of his contemporaries described him as impressively tall and, in middle age, very fat. (His students spread the story that because of his girth they had to cut a semicircle out of the table where he sat.) He was famous for the sheer intensity of his study and literary production—it was said that he had four secretaries to whom he would dictate simultaneously four different works. This devotion to the intellectual life was sustained by a deep devotion to liturgical and contemplative prayer.

Thomas was born near Aquino on the northwestern fringe of the kingdom of Sicily, governed by the Emperor Frederick II, who was in constant conflict with the pope. His influential family therefore sent him to the emperor's university in Naples. In this he was lucky, for sophisticated Muslim and Jewish scholarship had begun to penetrate Europe, and Thomas, guided by Peter of Ireland, now encountered the translations of the major works of Aristotle, which had long been lost to the West.

It was here, too, that he came across the new Dominican friars, who combined a vow of poverty with a life of prayer, study, and preaching. He wanted to join them, which involved a journey north. His family, who had thought of him as a future abbot of the prestigious Benedictine house of Monte Cassino, detained him forcibly, but after about a year of resisting their persuasions he was allowed to continue on his way to Paris. There he was to complete the major part of his greatest work, the *Summa Theologiae*.

There is a story that as a small child Thomas used to pester everybody by asking them, "What is God?" Certainly this question preoccupied him throughout his later life. He thought that there had to be an ultimate explanation of there being a universe instead of just nothing at all; but he also thought that, whatever this explanation might be, it must be beyond human understanding. The explanation we are looking for is an explanation of every-thing, which is why we cannot grasp it. We shall know God as he is only when he brings us beyond faith to the "beatific vision," a sharing in the Father's understanding of himself, when we share in divinity.

In the meantime, however, we can speak about God because at least we can know what the explanation of the universe could *not* be. For example, whatever God may be, he is not a god, one of those great natural forces that seem to tower over us. There is, and should be, no mention of God in textbooks of physics, because God's explanatory power does not stand alongside physical causes but is the constant source of all such causality. But what, then, about the causality of our free choices? Can there be any freedom in a world so absolutely controlled by God? Aquinas answers that we are free not because we are independent of God but because we are to some extent independent of our fellow creatures. This is because our life, our *anima*, or soul, is not only, as with our fellow animals, the principle of our inherited bodily structure and oper-ations but also of structures of symbols and language that we make for ourselves. That is why we are free.

So another thing we can say negatively of God is that he does not bring about sin. It is we by our free choice who do that, because we sometimes want trivial goods, getting rich at the expense of great goods like being just or compassionate. We do not sin because we love evil but because we do not sufficiently desire our own happiness.

As to Aquinas's doctrine of God, here the most exciting thing is what we learn by faith: that God the Son shared our life fully in order that we might not just be good human beings but should share the life of the Spirit, the life of God himself. Toward the end of his life, after returning to Naples, did Aquinas receive some sort of experience of that kind? While celebrating Mass, he had a vision in comparison to which, he said, all his theological works seemed to him "like straw"—a sentiment in entire conformity with his lifelong views on the mystery and near-ineffability of God; one that every genuine Christian theologian would wish to echo.

□

Herbert McCabe was a Dominican friar who taught philosophy and theology at Blackfriars, Oxford. He died on 28 June 2001.

Bridget of Sweden
(1303–1373)

by Roger Ellis

Better known in the century and a half before the Reformation than since, St. Bridget of Sweden has come under the spotlight again because of Pope John Paul II's decision to pronounce her a "co-patroness of Europe." She is renowned as the foundress of a contemplative religious order established "principally and first of all for women" and for using the (by then) uncommon form of a double monastery, under the leadership of an abbess, in which the monks provided the sacraments for the larger group of nuns. Bridget's early life was conventional enough. Born into one of the noblest families in Sweden and married at thrirteen into another, she was the mother of eight children; she was also active in the life of the court. After a pilgrimage to Santiago de Compostela in

1341–1342, Bridget and her husband Ulf took a vow of chastity, another indication of her religious spirit and the first step of the couple's proposed entry into religious life.

Ulf's death soon afterward launched Bridget on a very different career. In 1344 she received a revelation from God, the first of more than seven hundred in all. In this "summoning revelation," a kind of climactic conversion experience she shared with other medieval visionaries, God promised to make her his spouse and a channel for the expression of his purposes.

And so she set out to create a new religious order that would arrest the perceived decline in religious life across Europe and promote the spiritual regeneration of secular and religious authority. In order to secure papal approval for this project, she was directed to travel to Rome for the Holy Year of 1350 and to remain there until the pope returned from Avignon, the seat of the papacy since 1309. So a saint whose temperament led her to wish to found and enter a monastery was sent to the city that had become a byword for corruption and decadence. She waited nearly twenty years for the fulfillment of these divine promises: During that time, if we except journeys she made to centers of pilgrimage such as Assisi, she lived in Rome as a private citizen, following a regime of prayer and self-denial as close as possible to the one she had projected for her order and remaining unshakably orthodox in her beliefs.

The pope returned to Rome in 1367, but stayed only briefly before returning to Avignon. Worse still, he approved the creation of the order in 1370 in a form remote from Bridget's original intentions and much closer to existing monastic arrangements, which she had identified as part of the problem. She must have felt that all she had been struggling to achieve since her calling by God had come to nothing. Possibly in reaction to this disappointment, she spent the last year of her life on pilgrimage to the Holy Land. She never lived to see the full realization of her prophetic instincts: Only after the outbreak of the Great Schism in 1378, when her followers threw their weight behind the newly elected Roman pontiff and against the French antipope, was the order approved substantially as she had conceived it.

As a noblewoman—even from a country as remote from Rome as medieval Sweden was—it was much easier for Bridget to make her voice heard in the councils of the great: Think, by contrast, of the fires that threatened the bourgeois visionary Margery Kempe (1373–c. 1436) and burned the peasant visionary Joan of Arc (1432). Even so, she and her followers had regularly to confront head-on the charge that God would surely not have chosen an ignorant woman to make his purposes known. By this light, Bridget's decision to assume the role of a private citizen while following a quasi-monastic regime shows how she had to be seen to conform to the stereotypes of religious life that Rome could accept.

Her significance for the new millennium lies not in her many revelations nor in her exercise of the accepted roles of wife, mother, and widow—though this may have commended her to the present pope, as it did to Benedict IX when he canonized her in 1391; nor in her very original conception of the role of the nun; nor in her journeying around Europe as a pilgrim. Nor does it lie in her expression of the prophetic charism, at least not as prophecy is conventionally understood.

No; her greatest legacy, in my view, comes with those twenty and more years of waiting, and then afterward with the answer that appeared to run counter to everything she had given her life to. The twin experiences of waiting and failure make her more genuinely relevant to the lives of ordinary Christians entering the new millennium than almost anything else in her story.

□

Roger Ellis teaches medieval literature and creative writing at Cardiff University in Wales.

Gregory Palamas
(c. 1296–1359)

by Bishop Kallistos of Diokleia

Earth's crammed with heaven,
And every common bush afire
  with God;
And only he who sees
   takes off his shoes....

Elizabeth Barrett Browning's words sum up the standpoint of St. Gregory Palamas. He is indeed one who "sees" and "takes off his shoes," who is passionately convinced that "earth's crammed with heaven," that God through his divine energies is present in every place and fills all things. He is par excellence a theologian of Christ's transfiguration, who believes that the uncreated light of Tabor—the mountain where Christ's transfiguration took place—is all around us, within each person and each thing. The gate of heaven is everywhere. The greatest religious thinker in the last centuries of the Byzantine Empire, he is at the same time someone who speaks to our own day, an ecological saint, whose theology of transfiguration glory has direct relevance for the contemporary secularized West that has so tragically lost its sense of the sacred.

Gregory's life falls into three distinct periods. There is first his time of seclusion. Aged about twenty, he entered the monastic life on the Holy Mountain of Athos. Here he became a *hesychast*, one who pursues *hesychia*, inner stillness or silence of the heart. He learned to use the Jesus prayer, the short invocation "Lord Jesus Christ, Son of God, have mercy on me," frequently repeated. He was also told about, and almost certainly himself experienced, the vision of light that the Athonite monks sometimes received during prayer and that they believed to be nothing less than the divine glory of Mount Tabor.

Then comes the second period. The way of *hesychast* prayer practiced on the Holy Mountain was called in question by a learned Greek from southern Italy, Barlaam the Calabrian. In his view the radiance seen by the monks was no more than a physical and created light, a delusion produced by the physical techniques they adopted. Gregory came to the defense of the *hesychast* tradition, moving from Athos to the imperial capital. Three councils held at Constantinople (1341, 1347, 1351) vindicated Gregory's teaching, affirming that the light experienced by the *hesychasts* was indeed nothing else than the light that shone from Christ at his transfiguration. These three councils possess within the Orthodox Church an authority second only to that of the seven ecumenical councils.

Gregory lived at a time when the Greek East and the Latin West were drifting steadily apart, but he did not develop his theology of the uncreated light in conscious opposition to the Latin West. His understanding of transfiguration glory, so far from dividing Catholics and Orthodox, can help to draw them more closely together. It is part of a shared inheritance. The third period of Gregory's life begins in 1347, when he was appointed archbishop of Thessalonica, the second city of the Byzantine Empire. Here he took charge of a bitterly divided flock. He proved an effective peacemaker, with a burning zeal for social justice. So his life embraced both the desert and the city, both solitude and an active pastorate. He was proclaimed a saint in 1368, only nine years after his death.

As a mystical theologian Gregory was concerned to maintain, above all, three things. First, he is an existential or experiential thinker, who insists upon the primacy of personal experience. What matters for him is that we should each attain, personally and consciously, the vision "face to face" of the living God, and this he believes to be possible not only in heaven but in this present life.

Secondly, Gregory speaks of "the nearness yet otherness of the Eternal," to use a phrase of Evelyn Underhill. He places equal emphasis upon both the transcendence and the immanence of God. The Divine is mystery beyond all understanding, yet it is closer to us than our own heart. Like his Western contemporary, Meister Eckhart, Gregory employs the language of antinomy and paradox when speaking of God: "He both exists and does not exist"—God, that is to say, exists in a unique sense; he is not just one existent object among many—"he has many names and yet cannot be named; he is ever-moving yet motionless; in a word, he is everything yet nothing" [perhaps the meaning is clearer if we write "no-thing"].

To safeguard these two complementary aspects of divine reality, Gregory develops a distinction between the essence or inner being of God and his energies or acts of power. The essence signifies the divine transcendence or otherness, and as such remains unknowable to created beings not only in the present life but equally in the age to come. But the energies permeate the entire universe, and we humans can participate in them by grace.

Thirdly, believing as he does in the omnipresence of the divine energies, Gregory insists upon the intrinsic holiness of the human body and of the whole material creation. The divine light transfigures the bodies as well as the souls of the saints, so that they themselves become—in both soul and body—that which they behold. As he puts it, "The body is deified along with the soul." It is this that makes him distinctively a theologian for our own desacralized era.

□

Bishop Kallistos of Diokleia is Spalding Lecturer in Eastern Orthodox Studies at the University of Oxford.

Sergius of Radonezh
(c. 1314–1392)

by Sergei Hackel

The haunting eyes of Sergius stare at me from my book. The artist has shown them as ill-focused, even crossed. It is an image of 1422, the year when Sergius was proclaimed a saint, and it allows a peep behind the scenes. He had died only thirty years earlier, and new evidence could still be garnered. Artists and writers soon saw to it that that image should be tidied up. Sergius grasps a scroll. But were the scroll to be unfurled, it would not reveal selected teachings from his pen, for Sergius left no writings of his own. And yet his impact was immense. At a time when his fellow Russians were still disorientated after conquest by the Mongols, he was to revitalize monastic life and thus society at large.

Not that anything like this was planned. In his early twenties, Sergius had decided that seclusion would be needed for his chosen life of prayer. He did not have to go far: The forests near Radonezh provided him with "desert." Here he settled, with his brother Stephen. They built accommodations and an unpretentious ("Holy Trinity") chapel.

Sergius's formative years were to be spent in isolation, for his brother soon withdrew. A fifteenth-century *Life* describes his struggles with demonic powers, some of whom appear in Western (Lithuanian) garb. More congenial company was provided by a bear, with whom he shared his meager scraps of bread. These few years were to endow him with the sobriety, humility, and silence, from which he drew in public life.

For public life was to be thrust upon him. Individuals gathered round him in the wilds, and so began a loosely organized community that lasted fifteen years. Sergius was persuaded to become its abbot and its priest, although he was reluctant to be either. Nor was this a whim. In due course he was offered promotion as senior hierarch of the Russian Church and declined in no uncertain terms, asking: "For who am I, being sinful and the worst of men?"

His humility determined his appearance. Catching sight of an uncouth Sergius working in the gardens, a visitor said: "I came to see a prophet: All you show me is a peasant."

Yet his integrity was valued far and wide. A Byzantine bishop wrote, "I hear of you and of your virtues." These were to prompt a letter from the patriarch himself, which noted his spiritual achievements but also mentioned "one thing lacking": Could not Sergius establish rules for monks to live their life in common? That meant reverting to Byzantine norms, and in 1363 Sergius accepted the proposal, for which he must have been prepared. Most monasteries in Russia were to follow suit. No less than thirty-five were founded by adherents of the saint.

Not that the reform was welcomed by each and every monk. The patriarch was to upbraid anyone who raised objections. One of these was Sergius's brother, who had joined the community once more. When he overheard his plaints, Sergius simply went elsewhere and might have stayed away forever had not his bishop intervened.

Sergius's reform centralized all monastic funds and under-takings. Since the monastery attracted tax-free benefactions under Mongol rule, it was impelled to offer succor to anyone in need. "Never forget to entertain strangers" was a precept that Sergius used to quote until his dying day, in 1392.

It was not only church leaders who thrust a public role upon him, for Sergius's reputation also cast him in the role of diplomatic troubleshooter. Since his actions as agent of the Muscovite establishment hardly conformed to saintly standards, they were omitted from his *Life*. Other works extolled him as the public figure who blessed the prince of Moscow for his battle with the Mongol horde in 1380, although it is now less certain that the authors got it right. But they enhanced the image of the patriotic (or at least pro-Moscow) saint.

In dealing with the state, his was never a prophetic stance. When there were rival claimants for the headship of the Russian Church, one of the contestants questioned whether Sergius should be neutral: "Why content yourself with silence, when you see a holy place blasphemed?" Yet Sergius was content with silence.

His understanding of the new mystical currents that were penetrating Russia from the Byzantine world is poorly documented. But even in the overpolished *Life* of Sergius he may be seen as sharing in the light of Christ's transfiguration, which he encountered in a eucharistic context. His disciples spoke of a radiant angel concelebrating with him at the altar, and were ready to accept that Sergius should receive a visitation from the Mother of God herself, unprecedented though this was in Russian lives.

Sergius's vigils and his visions were difficult to chronicle. All the more important, therefore, are the insights provided by the monk Rublev, a painter of his entourage. Perhaps Rublev designed the portrait of the squinting saint? It was certainly he who painted the main icon for a new Trinity Church in which Sergius's relics were enshrined. The beauty of Rublev's trinitarian image of three angels has caught the world's imagination. Yet it could well have drawn on Sergius for its sacred balance, grace, and awe.

□

Archpriest Sergei Hackel of the Russian Orthodox Church (Patriarchate of Moscow) is editor of religious broadcasting at the Russian Service of the BBC.

Julian of Norwich
(c. 1342–c. 1420)

---

by Sheila Upjohn

When T. S. Eliot quoted Julian of Norwich in *The Four Quartets* in 1944, "And all shall be well, and all manner of thing shall be well," very few people could have said where the words came from. Today Julian is the best-known of all the fourteenth-century English mystics. *Enfolded in Love,* the little anthology of excerpts from her book, has sold over 100,000 copies worldwide and has been translated into many languages, including Korean and Japanese. Julian was by her own admission "an unlettered woman" who, on 8 May 1373, had a vision lasting several hours in which Christ appeared and spoke to her. She spent the rest of her life as an anchoress in a small room attached to St Julian's Church in Norwich, where she meditated on what she had been shown and wrote her book—the first by a woman in English. Why does it speak so vividly to us today?

Perhaps part of the reason is that—unlike the work of her great contemporaries—it was almost unknown in her lifetime, and so was not subject to censorship by the church. The long text survives in only three manuscripts, none of them contemporary— all copied out long after the invention of printing had made this labor unnecessary. Two of them contain this warning from the scribe: "I pray Almighty God that this book may not come except into the hands of those who wish to be his faithful lovers, and those who will submit themselves to the faith of holy Church...." There is only one contemporary manuscript—a first draft of the book. This disappeared for centuries, and was not discovered until Lord Amherst's library sale in 1909.

My guess is that only a few copies of her book were made and that these were passed around secretly among trusted friends. For although Julian continually asserts she is a loyal daughter of "holy Church," the fact is that the revealed Christ who spoke to Julian showed her many things that seemed to contradict the church's teaching. She writes:

> Now during all this time, from beginning to end, I had two different kinds of understanding. One was the endless, continuing love, with its assurance of safekeeping and joyful salvation—for this was the message of all the Showings. The other was the day-to-day teaching of holy Church, in which I had been taught and grounded, and which I understood and practiced with all my heart. And this was not

taken away from me, for I was not turned or led away from it at any point of the Showings. But I was taught, by this, to love it and rejoice in it so that, by the help of our Lord and his grace, I might grow and rise through it to more heavenly knowledge and higher understanding.

It is just these insights that speak to us today:

In God there is no anger, as I see it....He looks on his ser-vants with pity, not with blame....There is no hell except sin for a soul that is true to its nature....Just as he does not stop loving us because of our sin, so he wills that we should not stop loving ourselves or our fellow Christians....As truly as God is our Father, so just as truly he is our mother....God showed that sin shall not be a shame to man, but a glory.

All of this might be good twentieth-century theology—but would certainly have been ranked as fourteenth-century heresy.

If Julian's book had been known officially to the church in her day, not a word of it would have survived—and neither might she. She could have been burnt at the stake and the book thrown on the fire alongside her. So why does Julian's book speak to so many people today? I believe it is because we are ready for it; that in the six hundred years that have passed since that day in 1373 when the risen Christ spoke to her, we have come to understand that God is not looking for every excuse to cast us into hell-fire, but that he loves us and cares for us; and that, in spite of sin: "All shall be well, and all manner of thing shall be well."

□

Sheila Upjohn is the author of In Search of Julian of Norwich *and* Why Julian Now?

Catherine of Siena
(1347–1380)

by Tina Beattie

Catherine of Siena is a baffling and strange saint. Christ told her in a vision, "...you are she who is not...I am he who is...," but she was a strong-willed woman who spoke with authority in her own name. Obedience was a cornerstone of her spirituality, but she defied the authority of her parents and challenged the church's leaders. She practiced extreme asceticism, but she expressed her love for Christ in lavish metaphors of embodiment. Her mystical experiences seem bizarre, but her theology is the product of a highly rational mind.

She was born in Siena in 1347, the youngest of twenty-five children. At the age of six she had a vision of Christ in glory that inspired her to take a pledge of virginity, to the chagrin of her parents. At sixteen she joined a Dominican lay order, devoting herself to the poor and the dying. Catherine's reputation for spiritual wisdom attracted a circle of followers and gained her access to some of the most important people of her time. She is credited with having been influential in persuading Pope Gregory XI to return the papal court from Avignon to Rome, and she defended Pope Urban VI at the time of the Great Schism, when a rival papacy was established in Avignon. She died in 1380, grieving over the parlous state of the church and in physical torment after months of self-starvation. She was made a doctor of the church in 1970. Catherine's confessor and close friend, Raymond of Capua, wrote the *Life of Catherine of Siena* after her death, but the *Dialogue*, dictated by her, and the several hundred letters attributed to her give the best insight into her thought.

The essence of Catherine's spirituality is knowledge of self and knowledge of God. This self-knowledge constitutes an unflinching examination of the subtle ways in which love of self prevents the soul's union with Christ. Catherine has an audacious confidence in human nature, and the process of self-discovery is one of restoration and freedom achieved through prayer and self-discipline. Our longing for God originates in God's love for the human made in God's image, and through baptism we enjoy a liberating return to God. The baptized believer is always free not to sin, for Catherine sees sin as negation. "Sin," she says, "is nothing." Like Luther, Catherine recognizes that we are saved by faith alone. Our works are occasions for pride, which constitutes the greatest risk to our souls. God tells Catherine that the only unpardonable sin is that of the soul who at the end judges "her misery greater than my mercy."

Catherine expresses the unifying love between God and the soul in vivid eucharistic imagery. Sometimes she addresses God with a sense of awe, sometimes with almost teasing familiarity. "Oh, loving madman!" she exclaims at one point. Although she uses nuptial language, she depicts Christ more as a nurturing maternal body than as a sexualized lover. She is enviably free of the anxieties about gender that so inhibit the modern Christian imagination. Raymond of Capua describes having a vision of her as a bearded man, but Catherine told him that, although as a child she had considered disguising herself as a man, she was told by God that he would send her out as a woman, to shame immoral men.

For Catherine, as for modern liberation theologians, the Christian life entails solidarity with the poor, and she rails against the affluence of the clergy. She argues that union with God can only be expressed through love of one's neighbor. God says to her, "...every sin done against me, is done through the medium of the neighbor....So far as the soul loves me, she loves her neighbor." But her social radicalism is often tempered by pragmatism. Allaying the anxieties of a wealthy married man, she affirms marriage as pleasing to God and urges him to use his wealth for the good of others. This capacity for both pragmatism and extremism is also manifest in her attitude toward the body. While Catherine punishes her body for the sake of her rational soul, she also describes the body as the soul's companion, and looks forward to its resurrection, when "the soul will give bliss to the body."

Catherine was a woman of genius without status or education who dared to speak truth to power. In a letter to Pope Gregory XI she said that if he would not exercise his authority, "it would be better to resign." Much about her is repellent to the modern mind—her overblown rhetoric of sin, her self-mortification, her support for the Crusades. Yet Catherine shows us the essence of Catholic mystical theology. The mystics are not perfect human beings. They are those rare souls who have been transformed by the "fire of holy desire." We should not seek to emulate them, but allow them to kindle within us that same fire which brings each of us to the unique perfection of ourselves in Christ, and makes us divine.

❑

Tina Beattie is a writer and lecturer in theology. She has a special interest in women's issues and teaches courses on the women mystics.

Thomas à Kempis
(c. 1380–1471)

by Melanie McDonagh

In André Gide's little novel, *Strait Is the Gate*, the Protestant heroine, Alissa, shows her determination to turn away from the world and her lover by abandoning Pascal and the beautiful writers and taking up devotional literature. She ends up with just two books: the Bible and the *Imitation*. She doesn't need to spell out the title.

The *Imitation of Christ* has had an extraordinary, universal appeal. Written in the early fifteenth century by a religious for religious, it was read by Protestants as avidly as Catholics, and there were times when it was surpassed in popularity only by the Bible. It informed the spirituality of Calvin and the *Spiritual Exercises* of Ignatius Loyola and was daily reading for Pius XII.

In our own day, it is far less admired. It is not hard to see why: The self-abnegation, the contempt for the world, the insistence on personal sinfulness are Christian commonplaces, but they run against the grain of contemporary spirituality. One friend, a friar of conservative disposition, tried to read the *Imitation* for Lent but gave up: He couldn't stand the author's disrespect for learning.

Yet this little book still has the power to move a modern reader. As Father Ronald Knox (who read a chapter every day) wrote in *The Tablet:* "If a man tells you that he is fond of the *Imitation,* view him with sudden suspicion; he is either a dabbler or a saint." No chance of that in my own case, who can never read the section "About Useless Gossiping" without a hot blush. But in the *Imitation,* the practice of Christian virtue is only a means to an end—union with Christ, the Beloved, which is consummated in the Eucharist. What about the author? Don't ask. The controversy on this subject has lasted five centuries, and this deliberately anonymous work has apparently been attributed to no fewer than 365 writers, among whom the most serious candidates are Thomas à Kempis, Gerard Groote, and Jean Gerson of Canabaco.

Thomas is the likeliest author. He was born in 1380 in Kempen, near Cologne. He left home at thirteen to join his brother John, a follower of the remarkable Gerard Groote, in the Community of the Common Life in Deventer, northeast of Arnhem. This was a quasi-monastic society whose members lived together in poverty, chastity, and obedience, earning their own livelihood. As Thomas wrote later: "They were of one heart and mind in God...what each possessed was held in common, and being content with plain food and clothing, they took no thought for the morrow."

Thomas spent seven years with Gerard's successor, Florentius, whom he loved dearly. In 1399, he joined the new house at Mount St. Agnes and was ordained at thirty-three. He spent most of his life here, until his death from dropsy in 1471. His remains were removed two centuries later; probably from this time we get the horrible little story that scratch marks were discovered on the underside of his coffin lid—an Edgar Allen Poe touch that doesn't bear thinking about.

Thomas's life was humble—he rose to be steward. As the monastery's chronicler wrote:

> He copied out our Bible and various other books.... Further, for the instruction of the young, he wrote various little treatises in a plain and simple style, which in reality were great and important works, both in doctrine and efficacy for good. He had an especial devotion to the Passion of Our Lord, and understood admirably how to comfort those afflicted by interior trials and temptations.

Some of the brethren kept a spiritual diary, and the *Imitation* has sometimes been described as Thomas's edition of Gerard Groote's. It might rather be said that the *Imitation* is a product of the piety of a community, the core of which was the imitation of Christ, the model of humility. The antiintellectualism of the *Imitation* finds an echo in Thomas's brief life of the monastery cook, John Cacabus, who remarks: "Well do we find it written in the gospels, 'Blessed are the poor in spirit'...but nowhere do we find it written therein, 'Blessed are the Masters of Arts.'"

The book is a fruit of that extraordinary spirituality that we associate with the *Devotio Moderna,* a renewal movement with its origins in the Low Countries, stressing the inner spiritual life of the individual. The *Imitation of Christ* is not the unique insight of Thomas, but he brought to this strand of medieval devotion notable shrewdness in practical advice, as well as single-minded insistence on inner devotion to the passion. In modern terms, the *Imitation* is preeminently Christ-centered: hence, its appeal to Protestants and Catholics both. Thomas's indebtedness to other writers, including Augustine and Bernard of Clairvaux, is obvious; their voices blend with his in a philosophy that combines occasional mysticism, bracing realism, and great tenderness: "Lord, what can I rely on in this life?," the Learner asks the Beloved. "I had rather be poor for your sake than rich without you. I would choose to roam the world with you beside me than possess heaven and not you; but heaven is where you are, and where you are not—that is what death is, and hell."

□

Melanie McDonagh is a journalist based in London who has been studying for a doctorate at Cambridge.

Fra Angelico
(c. 1400–1455)

by Michael Adams

It is difficult in the whole history of European painting to find a work that outdoes in beauty, simplicity, and technical skill Fra Angelico's *Annunciation* on the landing that leads to the friars' cells in San Marco, Florence. The painting confronts you as you reach the top of the stairs, and in it you sense both the intensity of the moment and the reluctance of the young virgin to accept so tremendous a responsibility. She looks so innocent, so vulnerable; it is as though she is beseeching the angel to find someone else, someone more able to cope with this unprecedented command. And it is only when you have digested the painting's message and its significance that your attention turns to its apparently artless design, to the perfect balance of the composition and to the harmony of the color scheme, with the Virgin's deep-blue robe and Gabriel's pale rose one set against the plain stone of the walls and columns. And only then, perhaps, do you appreciate the skill with which the artist has depicted the graceful arcade, whose columns and arches go step by step into the background, in such a way as to lend depth and an impression of intimate space to the design. As a composition it is faultless, as satisfying to the eye as it is stimulating to the imagination. It is timeless, too, for though the ideas that animate it derive from the Middle Ages, the technique is modern and masterly.

No one has ever had a bad word to say about Fra Angelico. Living and working for most of his life in Florence, at a time when his contemporaries among the artists were men of the stature of Donatello, Ghiberti, and Brunelleschi, he showed no inclination to engage in the rivalries that enlivened the artistic scene in the early part of the fifteenth century. Nor, despite his great gifts, did he provoke the jealousy of others. This was partly because he confined himself as a painter almost entirely to the religious subjects that were the traditional mainstay of the Florentine painters, to which he brought what one critic has aptly called "his own original accent of pure unsurpassed candor." But perhaps most of all it was because of his winning personality, "so humble and modest," in the words of Vasari, who tells us that Fra Angelico declined the pope's offer of the archbishopric of Florence, protesting that he would never feel able, unassuming as he was, to rule over others.

Before he entered the Dominican order, he had trained as an artist, specializing in the decoration of illuminated manuscripts, and he was familiar with the stylistic innovations being introduced by Masaccio and others at this moment of transition from the Middle Ages to the Renaissance. Even some of his most characteristic work in the churches and convents of Florence shows, for instance, his perfect understanding of perspective, whose treatment so absorbed contemporary artists like Paolo Uccello.

Born Giovanni di Fiesole between 1387 and 1400, it is not clear when or by whom he was first called Angelico; perhaps it was a reference to the ease and familiarity and grace with which he portrayed angels in so many of his paintings. "Beato" too seems to have reflected the general assessment of his associates, both in the Convent of San Marco and among the artistic community of Florence. Ruskin paid him the equivocal compliment of saying that Fra Angelico "was not an artist properly so-called but an inspired saint," and it is not difficult to see what he meant.

But Ruskin, dare I say it, was wrong. Fra Angelico's saintliness was a part, and a huge part, of his personality as an artist; but to it was harnessed an outstanding grasp (or perhaps simply an instinctive understanding) of the technical aspects of his craft, which he expressed in purity of line, economy in composition, and an exuberant feeling for color that any artist in any age might envy.

There is irony in the fact that the great Convent of San Marco, acquired for the Dominicans by Cosimo de' Medici in 1436, rebuilt by Michelozzo and so reverently decorated by Fra Angelico, was to become at the end of the century the power base of the Dominican reformer Savonarola, whose ideas were so much at variance with those of the painter. The two of them were at one over the obligation to give absolute priority to the service of God, but where Savonarola's faith required of him and of the whole community the most severe austerity, Fra Angelico's approach was completely different. His faith called on him not to turn his back on the world but, like St. Francis whom he so much resembled, to welcome it and to rejoice in the flowers and the birdsong and all the other graces of an environment where, he had no doubt, God was in his heaven and all must be right with the world. It is that conviction, that happy confidence, that explains why Fra Angelico's work, with its sunlit simplicity, goes straight to our hearts.

◻

Michael Adams is a former Guardian *newspaper correspondent who has a special interest in Renaissance Italy.*

Martin Luther
(1483–1546)

---

by David Yeago

Martin Luther is usually credited with the rise of "modern individual freedom." It is a view supported by the best-known scene from Luther's life, at the Imperial Diet at Worms in 1521, when (as legend has it) a lone monk stared down church and empire and uttered defiant words in which the free modern individual first came into sight.

A closer look complicates this picture. Luther at Worms probably did *not* say the words everyone knows: "Here I stand, I can do no other!" What he undoubtedly *did* say suggests considerable ambiguity in his relation to modern freedom: "Unless I am convinced by the witness of the Scriptures or by clear reason...my conscience is captive to the word of God." The irony is rich: Luther is commemorated for emancipating the free modern individual, and that role is symbolized by an occasion on which he publicly declared himself...a captive. Just such ironies, however, mark his continuing spiritual challenge.

Martin Luther was a young professor at a backwater university when a modest pastoral initiative blew up in his face and irrevocably altered the course of Christian history. Concerned about the burgeoning indulgence traffic, on the eve of All Saints in 1517 Luther sent his archbishop a set of critical theological theses. Whether they were also posted on a church door is much debated; if they were, it was not a gesture of rebellion but an invitation to academic debate. But Luther's critique touched a sore spot in the contemporary church and sparked a crisis that rapidly escalated to European proportions, complete with charges of heresy and the threat of the stake.

By the beginning of 1521, Pope Leo X had excommunicated Luther, and Luther in turn was concluding that the papacy was the prophesied Antichrist—the "man of lawlessness" who "takes his seat in the temple of God, declaring himself to be God" (2 Thess 2:4). Arguably none of Luther's theological ideas has had more impact than his apocalypticism, which was also the background for his savage anti-Judaism, unquestionably his most grievous legacy. By his dramatic denunciation of the papacy, Luther helped shape a Protestant culture deeply marked by the traumatic discovery that institutions fail and authorities betray. Here Luther *was* undoubtedly an inadvertent progenitor of "modern individual freedom."

Yet in the end Luther is an uncomfortable patron for modern assumptions about self and freedom. His words at Worms strike to the heart of the matter, for such captivity is what Luther takes "freedom" to *be*. His freedom before the emperor was based not on his own inner resources but on God's domination of his conscience through the word. Freedom is not grounded in a power originating *within* the self but in a liberating dominion intruding from *outside* the self.

Indeed, if two words had to summarize Luther's spiritual legacy, we might well bypass the obvious "faith alone" in favor of *"extra nos"*—"outside ourselves." The way to life always leads outside the self. Or rather, the true self is not the ego we know by introspection, the bundle of fears, desires, and poses that asserts itself in "works." The true self is the self-in-Christ, the self *bestowed* from "outside ourselves" in the hearing of God's word. Thus Luther comments on Galatians 2:20: "Paul, as someone living in himself is altogether dead through the law, but as a person in Christ, or as Christ is living in him, he lives by the life of another, because Christ speaks, works, and carries out all actions in him." This brings Luther into tension with spiritualities that take as given a nuclear "inner self" seeking to unfold its potential from within.

Thus Luther is unusual in the positive role that "externality" plays in his thought. We are saved by Christ's coming through the "external" or "bodily" word and sacrament celebrated in local churches; the "outwardness" of Christian worship provides a concrete focus for the exodus "outside ourselves" to Christ. That local churches are mostly unprepossessing Luther knew full well; God has hidden his grace there, he believed, so that not the proudly "spiritual" but only the poor may find it.

Furthermore, faith for Luther is itself a *bodily* relation to Christ. By faith "there comes to be of Christ and us one body and flesh which we cannot divide, so that his flesh is in us and our flesh is in him, and he also dwells essentially in us…." This joining of our bodies to the crucified Christ underlies Luther's doctrine of the spiritual significance of worldly vocation, much more than any desire to "affirm secular reality."

The last words Luther put on paper were, "We are beggars. That's the truth." His drastic testimony to human poverty and overflowing divine grace, hidden in the ordinariness of the church and embracing body and soul in the self-giving of Christ, is not the spiritual counsel we rich Christians of the Northern Hemisphere are looking for at the beginning of the third millennium. But it is a durable word that will still resound when less astringent remedies have failed us.

◻

David Yeago is Michael C. Peeler Professor of Systematic Theology at the Lutheran Theological Southern Seminary in Columbia, South Carolina.

Erasmus of Rotterdam
(c. 1467–1536)

by James McConica

It seems doubtful that mainline Christians of any persuasion would place Erasmus on a short list of the great spiritual figures of the millennium, but that would be a pity. Though his passion for peace lingers on, apart from that he is thought of—if at all—as a mischievous intellectual whose most enduring contribution to the faith—the printing of the New Testament in Greek—was ultimately rendered obsolete by advances in biblical criticism. Otherwise he is best remembered as a satirist, and *The Praise of Folly* is the only work from his pen to endure long after the issues it addressed have been forgotten.

In truth, however, he was a crusading spirit, deeply committed and driven by intellectual passion into deep waters where ravenous theological predators abounded. Illegitimate at birth (about 1467), he was ordained as an Austin canon and lived his life between universities and printing houses, but he never found a spiritual family except in the international scholarly community whose purpose, like his own, was to revive Christian piety by restoring the sources of the faith and simplifying the devout life. Among these friends an intimate ally was Thomas More.

The key to the Christian vocation was in the New Testament, where (he insisted) the believer would learn "to know Christ and celebrate his glory." But he knew as well as any that Scripture could be a snare to the unwary, so it was vital that it be authentic and incorrupt, that it should be explained to the unlettered, and that it should be studied by the learned with a grasp of the original tongues and the world from which it had sprung. To accomplish this he wrote unprecedentedly erudite and extensive annotations on the standard Vulgate text, he wrote a new Latin translation that took his concerns with the Vulgate into account, and he wrote *Paraphrases* to guide the lay reader, which in translation found their way into every parish church in Tudor England.

All books are hostages to fortune. The Greek text of the New Testament was first published by Froben in 1516 as a last-minute addition intended for the few who could profit from it in coping with Erasmus's critical annotations. It was flawed but instantly famous. Used by Luther for his celebrated translation, it entered the mainstream of Protestant biblical scholarship, a mixed blessing for three centuries until the advent of nineteenth-century criticism, while his fresh and elegant Latin version was displaced by vernacular Bibles everywhere. The fruits of his textual study, embedded in the annotations, were absorbed anonymously—like so much of his educational and literary work—into the general stream of Christian culture.

Absorbed too was his huge output of pastoral and spiritual writing, as intimate a concern to Erasmus as was the promotion of Scripture to which it was an adjunct. Two titles are preeminent: the *Paraclesis*, his exhortation to the study of Scripture, and the *Enchiridion militis Christiani—Handbook of the Christian Knight*. In the former he urged that the Gospels "bring you the living image of his holy mind and the speaking, healing, dying Christ himself." The *Enchiridion* was a guide to the Christian life as lived in the world, with a strong Pauline emphasis, and urged, in place of monastic ideals, a life well led in the community and directed toward the renewal of the Christian polity. Yet, with its broad undercurrent of mystical theology, it served as a spur to the contemplative revival in sixteenth-century Spain. He wished to see the prevailing devotion to relics, pilgrimages, ritual penances, and other of the well-worn pieties of the day supplanted by active concern with charity, justice, social harmony, and the welfare of the whole. His proclaimed ideal—the "philosophy of Christ"— was of the city as a monastery, where an overriding aspiration to holiness was the concern of all the baptized, not simply of religious professionals. He was the great prophet of the lay vocation before Luther, but unlike Luther insisted on the subordination of the individual's judgment to the conscience of the wider community. His rule of faith, the consensus of the faithful through all ages, made his eventual disagreement with Luther inevitable and, in the end, it was Luther's perceived willingness to divide

Christendom over his personal convictions that led Erasmus to a public challenge.

His refusal to join either of the warring orthodoxies drove him late in life to exile from a radically Protestant Basel and to isolation within the Catholic community to which he stubbornly adhered. He died in Basel in 1536. For better or worse, his laicism, insistence on the equal vocation of all the baptized, on the unity of Christendom, on episcopal order and the essential role of the papal office, taken all together, make him preeminent among all the foundational figures of modern Christianity as the precursor of the Second Vatican Council.

□

James McConica, C.S.B., president of the Pontifical Institute of Mediaeval Studies, is a member of the international council directing the new critical edition of the complete works of Erasmus.

John Calvin
(1509–1564)

by David Fergusson

Although a leading reformer and a hugely influential theologian, Calvin remains an ambivalent, enigmatic figure. In part, this can be explained by a lack of detailed information about his early days and a characteristic refusal to draw attention to his own life. Both in temperament and background he differs sharply from Luther. Eschewing the expansive rhetoric of the great German reformer, Calvin displays the more measured tones of Renaissance humanism, allied to a theological conviction that the glory of God is above all else the theme of the preacher and Christian scholar.

Any genuine appreciation of Calvin's greatness has also to overcome the contemptuous terms in which he has been reviled (the term *Calvinist* in Scottish culture is often used for anything that is deemed judgmental, oppressive and authoritarian). Much notoriety surrounds his doctrine of "double predestination," which taught that God from all eternity had elected some for salvation while pre-ordaining the rest to everlasting damnation. Although Calvin pursued this with what one commentator describes as a "reckless consistency," he nonetheless understood himself to be expounding a belief that Augustine, Aquinas, and others had already taught. In any case, it never became a controlling principle of his theology.

Assertions that he advocated theocratic government and exercised an oppressive rule in Geneva are wide of the mark. He consistently maintained a division between the spheres of temporal and spiritual rule and found himself not infrequently at odds with the city magistracy. His complicity in the execution of the heretical Michael Servetus, though entirely reprehensible, was not egregious in the context of those barbarous times. And accusations that he belittled the world of the arts and the humanities must reckon with his own humanist learning, the contribution of his *Institutes of the Christian Religion* to the French language (a first edition was published in 1536 in Latin, with a French translation following in 1541), and the flourishing of education, scholarship, and culture in countries where the influence of the Reformation was greatest.

Born in northern France in 1509, Calvin trained in classics and law. While in exile in Switzerland on account of his sympathies with the Reformed movement, he was enlisted to serve the church in Geneva. The city eventually became his adopted home, and from 1541 he assumed a leading role in church and society there.

To many modern historians, Calvin's Geneva represents a cramped and monochrome model of society that had little scope for moral or religious pluralism. Yet his vision of social existence as dedicated to the honor of God has had important political and economic consequences. It has been described as the secularizing of holiness. According to the seminal study of the German economist Max Weber, *The Protestant Ethic and the Spirit of Capitalism* (1904), the Calvinist insistence upon a well-ordered, simple, and industrious life became a significant factor in the economic development of modern Europe. And the stress upon the freedom of the church to order its own affairs and the sinfulness of each individual provided powerful incentives toward a political order of checks and balances. Today, churches within the Congregationalist and Presbyterian traditions continue to appeal to his conciliar model of church government.

The details of Calvin's personal life are sparse. He married Idelette de Bure in 1540. Their only child, a son, died shortly after birth, and on his wife's death in 1549 Calvin was left to bring up two children from her previous marriage. He himself was dogged with chronic health problems. In his later life, he refers briefly to an experience akin to conversion some thirty years earlier. In his final months, he documents with meticulous care his illnesses, though little hint is given of his spiritual or emotional condition. His burial in a common grave without a tombstone sealed a self-effacing life.

Yet Calvin's career was marked by a startling literary output. Successive editions of his *Institutes* appeared, culminating in the final edition of 1559. This is the classical text of Reformed theology, although it should not obscure the far greater number of commentaries and sermons that Calvin also produced.

The sovereignty of God is a dominant theme of his theology, yet everywhere this is married to the notion of divine accommodation. God's glory is revealed not only in divine transcendence but in its reaching downward into the human condition. This is displayed above all in Christ's incarnation but derivatively in the gifts of Scripture, the church, its ministry, and its sacraments.

Much effort is given to articulating a doctrine of the real presence of Christ in the eucharistic elements to counter criticism that he undervalued the sacraments. His constant concern with ecclesiastical order in part reflects his fear of the anarchic religious trends of the time, but it is also born of an abiding sense of a mother church that nurtures, disciplines, and supports her children. In its display of both Reformed and Catholic trends, Calvin's theology remains a vital ecumenical resource today.

□

David Fergusson, a minister of the Church of Scotland, is professor of systematic theology at the University of Aberdeen, Scotland.

Ignatius of Loyola
(1491–1556)

by Michael Paul Gallagher

There have been various proposals to make a film about St. Ignatius of Loyola. I would suggest beginning the picture in 1550, a Jubilee year, with a panorama of the Roman skyline just after sunset. We would see the outline of the new St Peter's, without its dome, but with Michelangelo's "drum" under construction. Gradually the camera zooms in on a lighted window in a small building. Gazing at the sky is a bald man in his late fifties. Behind him one can glimpse papers covered with elegant handwriting. As the camera moves closer we realize that he is weeping quietly, and if the actor were good enough, we would know that these are tears of joy. Looking at the stars, Ignatius is overwhelmed by the glory of God. The papers behind him are his first draft of the Constitutions for his ten-year-old order, the Society of Jesus. Beside them is the first edition of his *Spiritual Exercises,* published in 1548.

In 1521, when he had his leg broken in battle and then experienced his dramatic conversion during convalescence at Loyola, he never imagined spending long years in Rome. Ignatius came from the Basque country and spent his youth as a courtier and only as a part-time soldier. After his conversion he thought of himself as a poor "pilgrim," a layman living on alms and offering spiritual advice to anyone who would listen. But he got into trouble with the Spanish Inquisition on account of his lack of theology. So at the age of thirty-three he went back to study ("to help souls"), learning Latin with small boys. His studies continued until he was forty-four. By that stage he had gathered several companions around him at the University of Paris, having led them personally through a month of guided prayer. They planned to go to Jerusalem together, but when that proved impossible they offered their services to Pope Paul III in Rome (eventually taking a special fourth vow of obedience to the pope "for missions"). Thus the Jesuits were born through a series of outer accidents, through the inner vision of this courtier turned contemplative, whose apostolic energy drove him to work both with princes and prostitutes.

Starting the film in that way would be an attempt to go beyond the misleading image of Ignatius as a severe soldier who founds an order of "shock troops" to combat the Reformation. His diary reveals another side altogether, symbolized by his weeping (which happened so often during Mass as to endanger his eyesight). The elegant writing sums up a man of courtly reverence, a quality that marked his relationship with God as Trinity. The Constitutions, over which he prayed for years, are unique in their emphasis on flexibility, giving priority to frontier ministries of different kinds. They embodied a nonmonastic approach to religious life and as such had a crucial influence on later "apostolic" religious congregations. The novelty of this approach no doubt gave Jesuits a more individualistic stamp than older religious families.

However, the greatest legacy of Ignatius lies in his *Spiritual Exercises*, which are more a set of instructions for a retreat director than a text to be read. I remember my disappointment—as a lay university student—when I borrowed the little book from a library. It seemed as ineloquent as a driving manual. But, as for many others through the centuries, it came alive years later when I "did" the thirty-day retreat. Ignatius drew on his own spiritual adventure to offer contemplative scaffolding for a succession of graces—trust, contrition, discipleship, freedom for the service of Christ. In this way the *Exercises* guide a retreatant through a pedagogy of prayer into "interior knowledge of the Lord."

Even though it was often interpreted in rigid ways, authentic Ignatian spirituality is marked by his typical preference for flexibility. His is a spirituality of discernment of choices, both everyday and lifelong. His advice is to find "whatever is most helpful and fruitful," and he tells the retreat director to get out of the way of God! To allow, in his surprising words, "the Creator to deal immediately with the creature." There is a fundamental trust here that the "movements" of the Spirit are recognizable in everyone's experience.

Secular history often speaks of Jesuit colleges as another major inheritance from Ignatius. They were not part of his original plan of a highly mobile ministry. But after 1548, when he was convinced of the importance of educational work, the schools mushroomed and evolved new ways of humanistic formation, encouraging for instance the writing of poetry and staging elaborate theatricals. Historians also stress the creative character of Jesuit missions, ranging from India to Paraguay—an outreach that started under Ignatius. But they should also mention times when Jesuits lost their roots and became inflexible and elitist.

What are the better hallmarks of the Ignatian tradition? Depth and practicality together. Order and adaptability. Contemplation and creativity. Remembering the mystic on the balcony, I think of Ignatius as outwardly controlled, inwardly emotional, and humanly a welcoming courtier. He welcomed history at a time of huge change—the outset of modernity—and he embraced change as the theater of the Spirit.

◻

Michael Paul Gallagher, a Jesuit priest, is professor of fundamental theology at the Gregorian University in Rome. He lives in the house where Ignatius spent most of his Roman years.

Thomas More

(1477–1535)

by Lucy Beckett

Most lay saints do not reach public notice. Thomas More led a life that was publicly visible for more than thirty years, its very visibility being a chief reason for its dreadful end. But his holiness was a quiet and private thing, evident to the world only in his death. "How many souls," Erasmus wrote, "hath that axe wounded which cut off More's head."

The England in which More was brought up, for all the shambles of the Wars of the Roses, which ended in shaky Tudor triumph when he was eight years old, had much stability and tradition to support a gifted boy whose father was a respected London judge. He went to the best grammar school in the city, at twelve became page to Cardinal Morton, was taught by Benedictine monks in Oxford, and then, at eighteen, finished his education at the Inns of Court, living for four years at the London Charterhouse and attending Mass and the Divine Office with the monks. After all this formation in the old institutions of the church, at twenty-two he made the surprising decision to marry—surprising because his upbringing had given him in many respects the soul of a monk, and surprising because his later intellectual friends—Erasmus, Colet, Linacre, Grocyn—were, to a man, priests.

As a lawyer, the first layman to be appointed Lord Chancellor, More was famous throughout Europe for the irreproachable integrity of his judgments and his judgment. As a classical scholar he was almost as famous. His *Utopia*, written in Latin for a cosmopolitan audience, was a *jeu d'esprit* derived from Plato's *Republic*, then unknown except to a handful of readers of Greek. It appears to recommend a utilitarian communism dependent on slave labor and mercenary soldiers. Christianity has not been heard of in *Utopia*, and the chilling uniformity of its citizens' principled but constrained lives has about it a timeless warning often missed.

A powerful reason for taking the book with a pinch of salt is that in *Utopia* nobody is ill or dies or eats or looks after children at home. More's first wife, Jane Colt, died, leaving him with four small children. He married again at once, a bossy widow, Dame Alice, with a child of her own. More's old father and various young wards also lived in his house. He was surrounded by this large, loving family, and his Chelsea household, recorded in

Holbein's wonderful portrait drawings, was renowned for its cheerful, peaceful atmosphere of piety and learning.

The girls were as well educated as More's son, and the whole family attended daily Mass and prayers, while More spent as much time as he could alone in his study. He wore a hair shirt under his velvet robes, and his life was as monastic as it was possible for a married layman's to be. Imprisoned in the Tower, he was not unhappy to be at last in an actual cell. As he told his daughter: "I find no cause, I thank God, Meg, to reckon myself in worse case here than in my own house. For me thinketh God setteth me upon his lap and dandleth me."

Between *Utopia* (1516) and More's death, Luther had rocked Latin Christendom; Protestants, excoriated and sometimes condemned to the stake by More, had begun to appear in England; and Henry VIII, in order to marry Anne Boleyn and legitimize her child as his heir, had, by a series of acts of parliament, abandoned the ancient authority of the pope and called himself "supreme head of the Church in England." It was the oath of supremacy that More refused to swear, together with John Fisher and the Carthusians who were martyred a few weeks before he was.

His family's failure to understand More's resistance to the king must have been the hardest thing for him to endure during his months of imprisonment. On 1 July 1535 he was convicted, on perjured evidence, as a traitor, under the Treasons Act of 1534, for "attempting to deprive the King of his title as Supreme Head of the Church." This he had certainly not done, but the king interpreted his resolute silence correctly: It was for his understanding of what the king had done that he was prepared to die and for this understanding that he was killed, "the King's good servant," as he said of himself on the scaffold, "but God's first." He died lightheartedly, not for freedom of conscience as some have said but for the unity of the church. He was writing in his last weeks a Latin essay, "On the Sadness of Christ." After the sentence "And they laid their hands upon Jesus," he put down his pen and left his cell for the block.

The execution won a small battle for Henry VIII but lost him and his successors an important war. More's death, soon compared by Cardinal Pole to the death of Socrates, was the inspiration of the recusants for a century and a half and has rightly haunted the memory of England ever since.

□

Lucy Beckett is the author of the historical novel about Tudor England, The Time Before You Die: A Novel of the Reformation.

Teresa of Avila
(1515–1582)

---

by Shirley du Boulay

Teresa of Avila was a most gifted and remarkable woman, who would score highly in a competition for most people's favorite saint. So varied were her gifts that it is hard to decide what makes her so significant: Should she be remembered primarily as a reformer of monastic life, as a theologian, as the gifted writer of many books, including *The Interior Castle*, or as someone who experienced and charted the mystical landscape in luminous detail? She was a captivating woman with a strong character—shrewd, practical, and determined—who spent her adult life as a nun in the turbulence of sixteenth-century Spain. She was only two years old when, in 1517, Martin Luther made his famous attack on indulgences and, though she understood little of the ideals behind the Reformation, she held strong views on the subject: As far as she was concerned it was quite simply wrong. She would, however, have been well aware of the Counter-Reformation launched by the Council of Trent.

Though she was distinguished by her noble birth, coming as she did from an old Spanish family, only recently has it become known that she was partly of Jewish descent at a time of fierce anti-Semitism, when the fear caused by not having *limpieza de sangre* ("purity of blood") was rivaled only by fear of the activities of the Inquisition.

She became a Carmelite, joining the Convent of the Incarnation in Avila in 1536 when she was just twenty-one years old, and her place in Carmelite history is assured, for the Discalced (or "Barefoot") Carmelites regard her as their founder. After some years in the convent she decided that life there was too easy and that the Carmelite Rule was not observed in its primitive rigor. Over the next two decades, in the face of considerable opposition and immense practical difficulties, not to mention the ill-health that dogged most of her life, she founded seventeen reformed convents, from Burgos in the north of Spain to Granada in the south.

For many years Teresa was tossed on a stormy sea of spiritual aridity and doubt; then, in her mid-forties, she was buffeted by waves of mystical graces—visions, raptures, and locutions. She was helped by her friend St. John of the Cross, whom she called "the father of my soul" and whose cool objectivity tempered her preoccupation with what was happening to her. These extraordinary experiences, coupled with her gifts as a writer, enabled her to chronicle the life of prayer, the stages between quiet discursive meditation and ecstatic union, with a clarity and insight that have never been surpassed. So widely admired is she as both writer and theologian that some ninety translations of her complete works have been made, and in 1969 she was proclaimed a doctor of the church.

She had the gift of simplicity and was able to use everyday imagery strikingly. A metaphor dear to her heart was water. Once her analogous garden is planted—in other words, when prayer life has begun—the plants need to be tended lovingly. This can be done in four ways, she writes. There is the laborious way of drawing water from the well, or the easier method of a waterwheel and buckets. The gardener's load is lightened if a stream runs through the garden, but best of all is rain, the natural source of water and one entailing no work at all on the part of the gardener. Then "there is no feeling, only rejoicing, unaccompanied by any understanding of the thing in which the soul is rejoicing." The highest union is beyond communication. The spiritual life is, of course, about our relationship with God, and this above all is where Teresa has so much to convey. The story of her castigating God for his treatment of his friends, ending with a tart "No wonder you have so few of them," is almost certainly legend; nevertheless, it captures the essence of her relationship with him, which was friendship. Friendship and communion with God are possible, she insists, and "this friendship is not remote but more sure and more intimate than ever existed between brothers or even between mother and child." She describes mental prayer as "friendly intercourse, and frequent solitary converse, with him who we know loves us." She was in continual conversation with God, receiving reassurance, chastisement, or hearing words that seem to complement her visions, for instance, "Now thou art mine and I am thine."

Her achievements, especially for a woman in sixteenth-century Spain, were remarkable; the mystical heights she reached were rare and exalted. Though capable of being hurt and envious, knowing disappointment and depression, she revealed the potential of ordinary mortals, proving that human frailty and sanctity can live together. She also showed that the deepest experience of contemplation is not incompatible with a busy outer life and practical achievements. Though she lived over four hundred years ago, we can relate to her as though she were alive today. She was, as has been said, "extraordinarily ordinary."

□

Shirley du Boulay is a biographer of Teresa of Avila.

John of the Cross
(1542–1591)

by Rowan Williams

Once someone has been pigeon-holed within the category of "mystic," it can be quite hard to see them again in terms of flesh and blood. John of the Cross has certainly suffered in this way: His extraordinary poetry is so concentrated in its lyricism that it is bound to give an impression of a man utterly consumed by inner fires; his prose, convoluted and repetitive and occasionally bursting out into turbulent passion, shows a human face, indeed, but tells us little about the particular struggles that shaped it all. A couple of anecdotes give us a bit more—the Christmas scene, John thinking he was unobserved as he picked up the wooden baby from the crib and danced around the room with it in his arms; or his insistence, when he took his novices into the country for meditation, that they go off alone, each one to look at God simply in the surrounding countryside. But the story of his life gives some very striking personal "depth" to all this; thinking of this or that episode, you may well say, yes, I see where that image, that turn of thought is anchored in the flesh and blood.

Unlike Teresa of Avila, his closest spiritual companion for many years, John's background was one of poverty and struggle. He lost his father at an early age, and the family was left destitute. As a teenager he helped support them by trying his hand (not very successfully, it has to be said) at various manual jobs. The nearest he came to steady employment was as a nurse and general dogs-body in a hospital in Medina for advanced syphilis and cancer patients. But with the help of a well-off patron, he managed to pursue some studies in his spare hours. His heart was already set on monastic life, and in 1563, at the age of twenty-one, he took his vows in the Carmelite house in Medina, with the name of Matthias. After study at the University of Salamanca, he was ordained in 1567.

By this time the Carmelite order was beginning to be stirred by Teresa's reform movement, and John responded enthusiastically to the call to greater poverty and simplicity (he had briefly thought of joining the Carthusians). In 1568 he and two other friars made their commitment to the reformed group in the order and set up the first male house of the reform at Duruelo. The years that followed saw several more foundations and a five-year period (1572–1577) as confessor to Teresa's convent in Avila. His influence on the development of the older woman was immense and can be clearly traced in the differences between Teresa's early autobiography and the masterpiece of her maturity, *The Interior Castle*. But bitter feeling between the two branches of the order was intensifying, and in 1577 John was kidnapped by representatives of the unreformed observance and imprisoned at Toledo for nine months.

His treatment was appalling—physical degradation, but also constant mental pressure. He suffered what we should now call consistent psychological abuse. His friends knew nothing of his whereabouts. And it was during this period that he composed many of his greatest poems about darkness, escape, the touch in the middle of the night of some unimaginable freedom. He escaped in August 1578, on the night of the feast of the assumption.

His scandalous experience helped to add force to requests for a proper and formal separation of the two parts of the order, and for some years John's life was externally easier. By the mid-1580s he had written most of his prose works and more poetry; the prose treatises are almost all attempts to comment on the poetry but keep breaking into a kind of poetry themselves, awkward and heated and intensely moving. In these years he began to mature his central theological insights as elaborated in *The Ascent of Mount Carmel*, as to how, in the ascent to God's light, every image and expectation of God is dissolved by God's own action—leading to a state of inner bewilderment, even horror, the "dark night of the spirit," which has to be diagnosed and treated with the greatest sensitivity by confessors and directors. And at the end of his life, in 1591, he was to experience yet again the external signs of such loss and humiliation, being stripped of his responsibilities in the order and abandoned by many former friends. He died in December 1591.

The impact of John in his works is painful, unforgettable, and decisive. Very few Christian writers have so plainly set out what it means to allow God to *be* God when we pray, and how this entails for us both total cost and total transformation. It is just the way things are that for God to be real to me I must shed my fantasies about him. If Jesus died in darkness, should we expect things to be easier for us? But his death was the supreme moment of union with God's act and desire.

John's Christian vision is not exactly one of cloistered virtue in the usual sense. It means most in just the places where it was born, the extreme places our age is all too familiar with.

□

Rowan Williams is the archbishop of Wales.

Mary Ward
(1585–1645)

by Lavinia Byrne

Mary Ward was born in Yorkshire in 1585. These were turbulent times for the recusant Catholic community to which she belonged. Her family home sheltered two of those involved in the Gunpowder Plot, the Wright brothers, her mother's brothers. Had she married, the intention would have been for her to secure the future for some notable Catholic dynasty, for her to breed a fresh generation of little martyrs.

As she saw it, "some other thing" was prepared for her. This insight came when she had already crossed the Channel to Flanders, to pursue an enclosed vocation as a Poor Clare, the only opening available to a devout Catholic woman at the time. St. Omers buzzed with the English exile presence: There were religious of every shade and hue and amongst them the Jesuits. Mary Ward soon fell under the influence of their charism. Here was a way of life that would enable her to journey into freedom, beyond the call of parental demands about a good marriage, beyond church demands about enclosure. Here lay freedom from the two emotional and self-imposed faults that so beset the female psyche. As she herself noted: "Vain fear and inordinate love are the bane of the female sex."

She had other things to say about women, too. In 1616, for instance, she harangued the growing community of women companions who had gathered around her. An unfavorable remark had reached her, reported to her by one Thomas Sackville, a visitor from Rome. "It is true," he reported, "they are in their first fervor; but fervor will decay and when all is said and done, they are but women." Mary Ward addressed her followers: "I would know what you all think he meant by this speech of his 'but women' and what 'fervor' is." She continued: "There is no such difference between men and women that women may not do great things. And I hope in God it will be seen that women in time to come will do much."

So what were the great things Mary Ward expected of her first companions? A desire to love and serve God in joy and freedom; the ability to prize truth; an apostolic spirit. As well as opening girls' schools in Europe, they would return to the mission field in England, for there were many families who would shelter active exponents of the Gospel; many homes in which she and her sisters could give the Spiritual Exercises of Ignatius to devout laypeople out of the glare of the public eye. They were in less danger than the missionary priests—though the archbishop of Canterbury said of her that she was "worse than seven Jesuits." Praise indeed. Not all the opposition came from such friendly sources.

Like many pioneers, she knew that the clarity of her own vision put her at risk. Her wisdom was out of kilter with that which prevailed in Europe after the Council of Trent. Yet she wanted something so simple: no enclosure, government by a woman general superior according to the Constitutions of the Society of Jesus, and freedom from any need to recite the Divine Office in choir. Each of these was an act of defiance as far as a besieged post-Reformation church was concerned. Her friends were numerous, but her detractors were more powerful. They had the ear of Rome and reported their concerns about the "galloping gurles," as she and her followers were called. Her opponents said: "The English ladies conform themselves to the ways of seculars. They are idle and talkative. They speak at meetings on spiritual matters, even in the presence of priests, and give exhortations, to which they are trained in their noviceship. They labor for the conversion of England, like priests. They want to be religious, but not monastic."

Which was the worst crime? Working "like priests" or "gadding about in town and country"? We will never know. All that we can be certain of is that Mary Ward pursued her tricky vocation through thick and thin. If we, in our own times, take the existence of modern apostolic women religious for granted, then Mary Ward and her first companions must be recognized as trailblazers: women who followed a star.

She died in obscurity in 1645 and was buried at St. Thomas's Church in Osbaldwick, outside York, where, we are told, the vicar was "honest enough to be bribed" to bury a Catholic. On her gravestone is written, "To love the poore, persever in the same,/ Live, dye and rise with them,/ Was all the ayme of Mary Ward." What was this "same" in which she persevered so courageously? It has been interpreted in many different ways, as indeed has her life. The happiest reading is a flashback to the vision that first put her on the road to freedom, when in 1611 she heard the words, "Take the same of the Society," and understood that to mean that she should aspire to adopt the Constitutions of the Jesuits and the spirituality of Ignatius's *Spiritual Exercises*.

Arguably, Mary Ward's is the first modern Catholic woman's voice. She wrestled with and wrote of things that still matter: the place of women in church and society; the life of faith; and our access to the divine will. Her spirit gallops on.

□

Lavinia Byrne lectures at the Cambridge Theological Federation.

George Herbert
(1593–1633)

by Philip Sheldrake

Prayer the Church's banquet, Angel's age,
God's breath in man returning to his
  birth,
The soul in paraphrase, heart in
  pilgrimage,
The Christian plummet sounding heav'n
  and earth;
Engine against th' Almighty, sinner's
  tower,
Reversed thunder, Christ-side-piercing
  spear,
The six-days world transposing in an hour,
A kind of tune, which all things hear and fear;
Softness and peace, and joy, and love, and bliss,
Exalted Manna, gladness of the best,
Heaven in ordinary, man well drest,
The milky way, the bird of Paradise,
Church-bells beyond the stars heard, the soul's blood,
The land of spices; something understood.

"Prayer" by George Herbert is one of the best-known poems in his collection *The Temple*. Herbert is a leading figure of seventeenth-century English literature, thanks to his prose treatise *The Country Parson* and his prolific poetry. He was also a major influence in the emergence of a distinctive Anglican spirituality, alongside other seventeenth-century poets such as John Donne, Henry Vaughan, and Thomas Traherne.

Herbert led a varied life before finally settling down as a country priest at Bemerton, outside Salisbury, for a short period before his death in 1633. He came from one of the leading aristocratic families, had been Public Orator of Cambridge University and a member of Parliament, apparently destined for a glittering public career. So his decision to seek ordination during the 1620s was a surprise. Herbert's inner struggles produced not only memorable writing but also a rich and deep spirituality.

Many elements of Herbert's spirituality are beautifully summarized in the poem "Prayer." A succession of metaphors tumble one after another to entice the reader beyond the expressible. Herbert offers many images of prayer, yet never *defines* it.

The poem begins with "the Church's banquet." At the heart of Herbert's spirituality lies the life of the church and liturgical prayer. Prayer is also spiritual food—a theme deepened by other metaphors in the poem, "exalted manna" and "land of spices." These allude to the Eucharist, and Herbert's eucharistic imagery is striking throughout his poetry. For example, the eucharistic banquet in his poem "Love" had a major impact on Simone Weil as the medium for her powerful mystical experience of Christ's presence.

Prayer is also "the soul's blood," the source of life within us, and "the soul in paraphrase," expanding us to our full potential. "God's breath in man returning to his birth" suggests that prayer has the capacity to return us to our first moment of creation, to a relationship with God that mirrors the experience of paradise.

The sensuous quality of the words suggests that prayer is certainly "softness and peace, and joy, and love, and bliss." Hints of inner struggle, however, save the poem from bypassing the painful complexities of human experience. "Engine against th' Almighty" describes prayer as besieging God. We battle with God and with our inner demons. In his sense of perseverance amidst spiritual struggle, Herbert echoes the Book of Psalms and the spirituality of early desert monasticism that were favorites of his.

George Herbert came to understand that the human heart, the "heart in pilgrimage," could be radically changed in prayer from a fear of God's wrath to a realization of God's loving acceptance of us in Christ. The graphic metaphor "Christ-side-piercing spear" reminds us of another poem, "The Bag." There, the Christ's wounded side becomes a space where we safely deposit messages for God.

"Heaven in ordinary," another powerful image of "Prayer," offers a rich vision of God within the everyday and yet beyond the ordinary. The mundane is transfigured by the radiance of divine glory. Interestingly, an "ordinary" in Herbert's time meant a menu of cheap food or the part of the inn where this was served or the people who ate such fare. This echoes another poem, "Redemption," where God, the "rich Lord," is not to be found "in great resorts" but amongst the "ragged noise and mirth" of the kind of disreputable people one might encounter in an inn.

Herbert's love of musical imagery appears often throughout his poetry—"Prayer is a kind of tune." "The six-days world transposing in an hour" suggests that prayer transposes the world into a different key and thus attunes us to a deeper reality behind surface impressions. In prayer, it is also possible to be transported to another realm entirely. "Angel's age," "the milky way," a tune "beyond the stars" suggest that prayer touches the infinite. Many people consider Herbert to have been a mystic. Certainly, for Herbert, prayer brings us into a profound, intense, and intimate relationship with God.

Yet the poem concludes with that elusive phrase, "something understood." These final words do not leave us with a definition. They are deliberately open-ended. In the experience of prayer there is merely *something* understood. It is tentative and incomplete rather than conclusive. The "understanding" is available to those who expose themselves to the risks of love. This "something" deepens our desire and presses us onward toward eternity. We sense on the margins of awareness the hope and promise of a final resolution, the ultimate seeing and hearing that Herbert's poem celebrates.

◻

Philip Sheldrake is academic director of Sarum College and honorary professor at the University of Wales, Lampeter. He is author of Love Took My Hand: The Spirituality of George Herbert.

Blaise Pascal
(1623–1662)

by Alain Woodrow

Blaise Pascal was a philosopher, physicist, and mathematical genius. But for Christians he is revered above all for his *Pensées*, fragments of a Christian apologia published posthumously.

A child of his time, he was excited by the new discoveries being made in the field of science. When he was twelve, he discovered the first thirty-two propositions of Euclid's geometry by himself and by the time he was sixteen he had written a treatise on conic sections.

The family then moved from Clermont in the Auvergne to Rouen, where it came under the influence of Jansenism, the austere mystical movement that was sweeping the French intelligentsia. This doctrine of Cornelius Jansen taught that without a special grace of God, reserved for the elect, the performance of the commandments is impossible. Since the operation of this grace is irresistible, human beings are victims of determinism, or predestination. This theological pessimism gave rise to austerity and moral rigorism and an attraction to the disciplinary practices of the primitive church.

Such was the "first conversion" of Blaise Pascal. But when his sister Jacqueline entered the Jansenist convent of Port-Royal in Paris, her brother opposed her decision. Loath to renounce the world and the admiration of his peers, Pascal pursued his scientific experiments and continued to enjoy his eminent position in Parisian society.

His "definitive conversion" took place on 23 November 1654. He was praying alone in his room by the light of a single candle, when suddenly the room was filled with fire. It was not simply a light but a fire, like the burning bush, which seared his heart and soul, Pascal recounted later. He saw God, in the form of a flame that consumed him with great sweetness. The vision lasted two hours, during which Pascal shed tears of joy. When it was over, he took a sheet of parchment and scribbled feverishly a record of his night of ecstasy. It began: "Fire. The God of Abraham, the God of Isaac, the God of Jacob, and not of philosophers and men of science. Certainty. Certainty. Feeling of Joy and Peace. The God of Jesus Christ.... Joy, Joy, Joy, Tears of Joy." He then sewed this "memorial" into the lining of his clothes, and carried it with him until his death.

From 1655 he was a frequent visitor at Port-Royal-des-Champs in the valley of Chevreuse, where Jansenist converts and sympathizers could meditate in seclusion. In support of the rigorous Jansenist morality Pascal battled against its opponents, the Jesuits, taking issue with the casuistical approach they favored in eighteen *Lettres écrites à un Provincial*, published anonymously in 1656 and 1657.

In 1656, another event in Pascal's religious life led him to turn from polemics to apologetics. His niece Marguerite Perier, who suffered from a fistula in one eye, was cured miraculously by the application of a relic of the passion, the Holy Thorn. Greatly impressed, Pascal decided to devote the rest of his life to the composition of an apologia of the Christian religion, addressed to the indifference of the *libertins* (freethinkers) who, though insensible to philosophical reasoning, might be convinced by the presentation of facts, the fulfillment of prophecy, and an appeal to the heart.

Even here, Pascal reasoned as a mathematician, producing as his trump card his famous wager. "To lose a golden sovereign is of little consequence, and yet one moves heaven and earth to find this earthly treasure. How then can one contemplate the loss of one's most precious possession, one's immortal soul?" In other words, it is in one's rational interest to act as if God exists, since the bliss of heaven and the infinite punishments of hell, provided they have a positive mathematical probability, however small, outweigh any countervailing advantages here on earth.

But the *Pensées* are read today not for their apologetic force but for their brilliant style and, above all, as a moving testimony to Pascal's personal experience and psychological insights. ("Man is no more than a reed—but he is a thinking reed.") He did not live to publish his great work, but left thousands of fragments, notes scribbled on bits of paper regardless of sequence, which were assembled by his friends and published posthumously in 1670, eight years after his death.

Pascal's writing is wholly centered on the person of Christ as Savior and obsessed by the tragic situation of humanity, placed between greatness and misery. ("What are we in the universe? Nothing compared with infinity, everything compared with nothing, we stand in between nothing and everything.") Pascal's anguish is evident—*"le silence éternel de ces espaces infinis m'effraie"* ("the endless silence of infinite space terrifies me").

Only faith can free him from this dramatic situation, since human existence is summed up by one crucial choice, a decision for or against God. A choice that springs from the heart, not the brain, for *"le coeur a ses raisons que la raison ne connaît point"* ("the heart has its reasons that the mind knows nothing of"). Pascal's God is not the God of philosophy or science, but *"un Dieu sensible au coeur"* ("a God who speaks to the heart").

□

Alain Woodrow was for twenty years religious-affairs correspondent of the French national daily Le Monde.

John Bunyan
(1628–1688)

by N. H. Keeble

John Bunyan's *The Pilgrim's Progress* is the most successful work of popular Christian theology ever published. No other committed Christian work of any persuasion from any period has enjoyed such an extensive readership. This is the more extraordinary since its author enjoyed no advantages of educa‑tion, cultural experience, or social position.

He was born at Elstow, Bedfordshire, in 1628, the son of a brazier (or "tinker"), whose trade he followed. He warns the readers of one of his books that they "must understand...I never went to School to Aristotle or Plato, but was brought up at my father's house, in a very mean condition, among a company of poor Countrey‑men."

In thus openly advertising his ignorance, Bunyan was defiantly claiming as a strength what might be supposed a disabling weakness. In the spirit of St. Paul in I Corinthians 2, he rests his homiletic and pastoral authority not upon his acquisition of "man's wisdom" but upon divine inspiration and the experience of grace. In a telling phrase, Bunyan declared that he "preached what I felt, what I smartingly did feel, even that under which my poor Soul did groan and tremble to astonishment." Urgent immediacy and personal conviction are hence characteristic of all he wrote.

Bunyan's Christian conviction was hard-won. In 1644 he was mustered in the parliamentary army and stationed at the Newport Pagnell garrison. Contact with Puritan radicals during the next two years was perhaps in part responsible for the ensuing period of intense introspection and spiritual crisis that he later recounted in the classic spiritual autobiography *Grace Abounding to the Chief of Sinners* (1666). Bunyan may have judged his sins more harshly than we would be inclined to do, but there is no questioning the confessional honesty with which he records the emotional and spiritual agony of his struggle to achieve assurance of saving faith.

Relief came to him in large part through the pastoral wisdom of John Gifford and the support of the independent Bedford congregation to which Gifford ministered. Soon after joining this church in 1654 Bunyan began to gain a considerable reputation as a preacher. Following the Restoration of Charles II in 1660, his was one of the Puritan voices that the restored regime moved quickly to suppress. He was arrested in the autumn of 1660 and, refusing to give guarantees that he would desist from preaching, he remained a prisoner (though with occasional freedom of movement) for twelve years. No longer able to preach by word of mouth, Bunyan did so through writing. His many prison books include both *Grace Abounding* and *The Pilgrim's Progress* (published in 1678, with a second part in 1684). He also maintained his contact with the Bedford congregation and, in January 1672, shortly before his release in March, he was chosen to be its pastor.

Altogether Bunyan published sixty books, but it is with *The Pilgrim's Progress* that he is identified. The controlling metaphor of this allegory he took from the interpretation of the Abraham legends in Hebrews 11:13–16 (they "confessed that they were strangers and pilgrims on the earth" seeking "a better country, that is, an heavenly").

This idea of the journey to salvation had been handled by many earlier Christian writers, but Bunyan developed it with a sharply observed realism, both psychological and circumstantial. We travel along a muddy, poorly signposted seventeenth-century road, over the Hill of Difficulty, through the Slough of Despond and the Valley of Humiliation, exposed to inclement weather, sobered by the sight of criminals' skeletons hanging from a wayside gibbet, apprehensive of footpads, grateful for the refuge of an inn or house hospitable to travelers. And walking this road we meet ordinary people with ordinary concerns.

It is Bunyan's engagement with actual human experience that gives his allegory its distinctive authenticity: We recognize the complacent Mr. Worldly Wiseman, the foolhardy Ignorance, the trying Mr. Fearing, as we do the quirks and follies of all the other pilgrims, rendered always in a direct and colloquial prose that has the very note of actual conversation. We recognize, too, Christian's own predicament. Bunyan's theology was predestinarian and Calvinist but it is experiential uncertainty, not metaphysical certainty, that his writing registers. In *The Pilgrim's Progress* Christian may receive his scroll, testifying to his election, but the outcome of his journey is hardly a foregone conclusion from his point of view. He is constantly beset both by external hazards and temptations and by his own recurrent anxieties and fears concerning the firmness of his faith.

Bunyan's great strength is to present a credible and an attainable model of holy living. It is because he recognized that faith is inextricably bound up with the imperfections of fallen human nature that his depictions of Christian and his wife Christiana offer encouragement to every believer troubled by inadequacy. His aim is to "make a Traveler" of his reader along the way to the Heavenly City, which lies open to every person of faith but runs unavoidably through the wilderness of this world with its vicissitudes, uncertainties, and moral complexities, until all the trumpets sound on the other side. That is both the book's challenge and its reassurance.

□

Professor Keeble is head of the department of English studies at the University of Stirling and has published extensively on Bunyan and on seventeenth-century Puritan writing.

George Fox
(1624–1691)

by R. Melvin Keiser

Founder of the Society of Friends—or the Quakers, so-called since they trembled at the Word of God—George Fox was a religious and social revolutionary. He believed that the real presence of Christ was to be found not in the "steeple house" but inwardly, in the heart and conscience of everyone, in the "true light that enlightens every man." For him, this inward divine presence spoke through the conscience to transform the world, not only religiously but socially, politically, and economically. His spirituality thus combined contemplation and action.

The child of a weaver father and a mother "of the stock of martyrs," at first he made a living through working for a shoemaker. But at the age of twenty-two he left home to wander in search of a spiritual meaning that he felt was absent in the Puritanism in which he had been raised. His criticism of the Puritans was that they believed righteousness was imputed to them by Christ's sacrificial death but was not actually made present in the human heart. Of that time he says in his *Journal:* "I fasted much, and walked abroad in solitary places many days, and often took my Bible and went and sat in hollow trees and lonesome places till night." In 1647 during the Civil War, when Oliver Cromwell was stirring up new religious fervor, he was brought to the edge of despair, for he realized that he had "nothing outwardly" to help him.

In this state he had a direct experience of God telling him: "There is one, even Christ Jesus, that can speak to thy condition." He "saw the infinite love of God" overcoming the world's evil, "an ocean of darkness and death," by "an infinite ocean of light and love, which flowed over the ocean of darkness." Joy filled him. A year later he experienced in a vision a return to the Garden of Eden: "Now was I come up in spirit through the flaming sword into the paradise of God. All things were new, and all the creation gave another smell unto me than before, beyond what words can utter."

These visions called him to a life of constant travel and preaching. From moment to moment, as he understood it, he was led by the Inner Light of the living Christ. He crossed England many times, accepting hospitality when offered, but often sleeping out in hedgerows. At the age of forty-five he married Margaret Fell, who was fifty-five, but spent little more than a week with her before continuing his travels, which took him through Scotland, Wales, and Ireland, Holland and Germany, America and the West Indies. He sought by his preaching to awaken people to that Light within, so that they would be purged by it and obey it as their primary authority in every instance.

As he preached, people were "convinced," to use the Quaker word, and by 1690 the movement had between 40,000 and 60,000 followers in England. He used his skills as an organizer to shape them into a collaborative polity, which came together in meetings held each month and quarter, and nationally in a yearly meeting, thereby removing himself from the center of authority. Everyone was enfranchised by his decision-making procedure that depended on the consensus of all the participants as they were led by God.

Fox abolished all traditional outward forms of worship— set liturgy, sacraments, Bible readings, singing. Instead, the people were to gather together in silence for common meditation and worship with no leader but the Spirit. From this issued a radical equality of women, who shared equally with the men, a revolutionary innovation at the time. Women flocked into the movement and became leaders, traveling as the men did. The most extraordinary traveling minister was Mary Fisher, a servant woman, who went alone to see the Sultan of Turkey to witness to "that of God"—as the Quakers put it—in him.

For Fox, religion and ethics were inseparable. He attacked social hierarchy through the use of the familiar "thee" and refused to doff his hat to his supposed superiors, to wear expensive clothes, to pay tithes supporting the established church, to use titles, to bow, or to flatter.

He was aggressive and argumentative in "speaking truth to power"—another Quaker phrase. He threatened the establishment both under Cromwell and under Charles II with his demands for justice and by the example of his followers, whose lives were transformed and deepened by their beliefs. Fox and his followers were militant but nonviolent. Their pacifism meant that they would not take up physical weapons against anybody; rather, the warfare in which they were engaged was spiritual, the achievement of depth within and justice without being the victory they sought.

Such efforts to establish social justice, to awaken people to the divine spark within them, and to create an alternative form of worship and church structure brought Fox grievous suffering. He was often beaten for speaking in church or interrupting the service and was imprisoned eight times. Physically robust, he experienced God's healing power coursing through his body after terrible blows and was known as a miracle-worker who was able to cure others of physical and mental ailments.

He has left words in his *Journal*, letters, and other writings that are incendiary, touching Quakers and non-Quakers with their evocative power. He knew, however, that it is not only words that speak, but lives. He practiced what he preached, providing a model in his own life and calling others to "be patterns, be examples in all countries, places, islands, nations, wherever you come; that your carriage and life may preach among all sorts of people, and to them. Then you will come to walk cheerfully over the world, answering that of God in every one."

□

R. Melvin Keiser is professor of religious studies at (the Quaker) Guilford College, Greensboro, North Carolina.

Johann Sebastian Bach
(1685–1750)

by David Maw

The *St. Matthew Passion* of Johann Sebastian Bach was considered by Mendelssohn (whose revival of it in 1829 secured the composer's reputation) to be "the greatest of Christian works." It is also one of the greatest of all musical works, demonstrating technical mastery and a genius for stylistic synthesis through its combination of intricate contrapuntal writing, dramatic recitative, emotive arioso, dance style, and the Lutheran chorale. Dating probably from 1727, it is the later and grander of Bach's two settings of the passion. Its use of a double choir and double orchestra enables a wide range of effects: the opening chorus is massive, with dense contrapuntal writing for choir and orchestra offset by the chorale *"O Lamm Gottes, unschuldig"* (the Lutheran

Agnus Dei) sung by ripieno trebles; by contrast, the aria *"Aus Liebe will mein Heiland sterben"* employs a texture of great delicacy, the soprano soloist being supported by an accompaniment of flute and two oboes.

Never before had such a range of compositional knowledge and such a depth of musical feeling been put at the service of church music. In the *St. Matthew Passion*, Bach reveals his own feelings about the passion story in music of the greatest emotional intensity, which he reserves for the aria *"Erbarme dich."* In the preceding recitative, Peter realizes that he has thrice denied Christ, as predicted. The aria begs mercy of the Lord, confessing the bitterest remorse. By a masterly stroke, Bach avoids obvious dramatic realism, giving the aria not to Peter but to the alto soloist. Thus, in a way characteristic of the tendency of the whole work to contemplation, the aria transcends merely personal reflection of Peter's state to become a regretful expression of human weakness with which all may identify. The voice is set against an accompaniment of sustained strings, the texture that accompanies Christ elsewhere in the work; so the aria is also the plea of Christ, now abandoned even by his closest disciple. Above the strings and voice, a solo violin plays one of Bach's most plangent, rhapsodic melodies in the melancholy rhythm of the *siciliano*. Perhaps in hearing this, we perceive the grace of God before human frailty.

Despite the majesty and mystery of his music, Bach's life was mundane and uneventful. He was born in the German town of Eisenach in 1685. Unlike his more cosmopolitan contemporary Handel, he traveled little and was better known in his lifetime as an organist than as a composer. Typically for the large musical family into which he was born, his career comprised a series of court and church posts in which he acted as a general musical factotum: composing, arranging, conducting, teaching, and playing organ, harpsichord, and violin. He worked in Arnstadt, Mühlhausen, Weimar, Cöthen, and Leipzig, and this last appointment, as cantor at St. Thomas School and director of music at the town's main churches, was the longest, lasting for twenty-six years.

Little is known of Bach's private life and character. He was twice happily married (his first wife died in 1720) and he had twenty children, several of whom became leading musical figures of the next generation. Apart from some youthful indiscretions at Arnstadt—including involvement in a brawl and a reprimand for inviting an "unfamiliar maiden" into the choir loft—and periodic wrangles with the town council at Leipzig, he seems to have been a reliable and conscientious employee. Nonetheless, though mindful of his inferior social position, he was not afraid to fight his ground when necessary on issues of pay and conditions.

He died in Leipzig in 1750, leaving amongst his effects a significant number of theological books. These demonstrated deep commitment to the Lutheran faith, and in his copy of Abraham Calov's annotated version of the Lutheran Bible, he had added comments in the margins and underlinings for his own use. One of these comments reads: "NB. Where there is devotional music, God with his grace is always present." What an insight into the composer whose artistic legacy includes more than two hundred cantatas.

Despite Bach's Lutheranism, his music has become a powerful expression of religious commitment to people of all denominations and faiths. In part this derives from his assimilation of a wide range of styles: secular dance and instrumental styles with the sacred Catholic polyphony of Palestrina and the simple pious melodies of the Lutheran chorale; but here he was merely fulfilling and extending the typically Lutheran rhetorical question: "Why should the devil have all the best tunes?"

In several works written toward the end of his life—*The Goldberg Variations, The Art of Fugue, A Musical Offering*—Bach explored to an ultimate degree the technique of music as an abstract expression of the human spirit. The last work in this series was the Mass in B Minor, a full setting of the Latin Mass compiled and adapted from earlier compositions. In its complete form, it would have had no natural home in the Lutheran liturgy; instead, it stands as a musical last testament. Through it, Bach professes the metaphysical truth of the art of composition as a reflection of the divine order that transcends historical circumstance and the differences between particular faiths.

□

David Maw a lecturer in music at Oriel and St Catherine's Colleges in Oxford.

John Wesley
(1703–1791)

by Leslie Griffiths

To understand the essence of Methodism in its first flush, you have to shut your eyes and use your imagination. Just think of a well-dressed clergyman of the established Church of England addressing a crowd of uneducated coal miners in the open air, an unheard-of phenomenon. He didn't do this naturally: He had to force himself to stand there and "become more vile," as he recorded it in his *Journal*. The miners themselves were startled and greatly moved at such attention. As they heard of God's love for them, many of them broke down and wept. Their tears traced white lines on their blackened faces. It was a moment of grace, and such incidents happened time and again across the length and breadth of the British Isles as John Wesley took his message to the masses. He rode thousands of miles, improvised pulpits wherever he could, and commended Christ to any who would give him a listening.

Wesley bestrode his century like a colossus. The claim is still made in some quarters that he, almost alone, saved Britain from a revolution similar to the one that took place in France. Reviled at the outset of his ministry, he was widely honored and revered at the last.

There was little in his beginnings to suggest what was to come. His family was well connected but very poor. Both his grandfathers had been dissenters, ejected from their livings in 1662. His mother had developed definite Jacobite sympathies, which might explain why the family's well-connectedness did not lead to preferment. It meant that John Wesley was born in a rural backwater, Epworth in Lincolnshire. His mother scrimped and saved to send him back to London, where he was educated at the Charterhouse school before going to Oxford, his younger brother Charles following a few years later.

It was at Oxford that the Wesleys forged a group of young zealots who were so diligent and organized in sharing their time between devotional, pastoral, and academic pursuits that they were mockingly referred to as "Methodists," a nickname that stuck.

The young Wesley was extremely devout. Out of his zeal, he undertook a mission to the newly founded colony of Georgia in America, where he hoped to convert the Native Americans and help to establish a Christian utopia. It was an utter disaster; Wesley had to cope with personal failure both in his missionary work and also in his first serious attempt to woo a woman.

During his voyage to Georgia, he had observed at close quarters the simple and trusting piety of some Moravians, a group of pious Christians from central Europe. They had remained calm during a storm when everyone else, Wesley included, had started to panic. He began to desire their capacity to trust; his quest led, in May 1738, at the age of thirty-five, to his conversion. His heart, he wrote, "was strangely warmed." His brother Charles had also been converted and now the Methodist movement could begin. The younger brother began writing a constant stream of hymns that have survived the centuries and are sung today across the Christian denominations: hymns such as "Love Divine All Loves Excelling," "Hark the Herald Angels Sing," and "O Thou Who Camest from Above." Catholics may finger their beads, Anglicans thumb their prayer books, and Quakers lose themselves in silence, but Methodism was born in song, and its sons and daughters have always sung their piety and their theology.

This centered on the doctrine of the universality of grace. "For *all*, for *all*, my Savior died," his brother had written. No Calvinist he. Allied to this catholic view of grace was the teaching on holiness: The justification of the sinner is never the end of the life of faith, but rather, its beginning. For the true believer treads a path of perfection, grows in love, dedicates his or her life to good works; a true Christian must walk the talk. All this smacked of "justification by works" to some of his Protestant contemporaries, and he was roundly accused by many as "a Jesuit fox." But Wesley remained unshakable: his teaching issued inevitably in what he called "practical divinity"; the only holiness he understood was social holiness. Schools, orphanages, health-care schemes, the relief of poverty, literacy, and campaigning for justice—all these were the practical outcomes of his theological understanding.

Wesley's organizational skills reached the levels of genius, with laypeople being used widely for preaching and pastoral care. The movement thrived in the urban sprawls created by the Industrial Revolution. At his death, there were some 70,000 Methodists in England, rather more in America.

It was America that contributed to the eventual separation of the Methodists from the Church of England. After the wars of independence, with British rule over, the pastoral care of the people of America remained (incredibly) in the hands of the bishop of London. An established church typically moves at the pace of a lame tortoise, and Bishop Lowthe refused to send priests to the renegade Americans despite much pleading by Wesley and others. Finally, in sheer desperation, Wesley ordained some of his own preachers and sent them to work in the United States. The die was cast and the seeds of a separate Methodist Church were sown. It was a tragic moment in church history.

Wesley died on 2 March 1791, full of years and firm in his faith. His last recorded words were, "The best of all is, God is with us." He was laid to rest in the graveyard of his beloved New Chapel on London's City Road. The final letter he wrote, less than a week before his death, was to William Wilberforce. In it he urged the young man to commit all his energies to "the glorious enterprise of opposing the execrable villainy" of slavery. That little phrase, shot through with a burning desire for justice, gives a true picture of the spirit of John Wesley, evangelist and social reformer.

□

Leslie Griffiths is the minister of Wesley's Chapel, City Road, London. He is a former president of the Methodist Conference and a writer and broadcaster.

William Blake
(1757–1827)

by Jill Paton Walsh

William Blake, among the finest poets in the English language, was at once a mystic visionary, like a medieval Catholic saint, and a kind of natural Protestant, a hero of independent personal thought. "I must invent a system," he said, "or be enslaved by another man's."

Born in London in 1757, the son of a hosier, he was apprenticed to an engraver and studied at the Royal Academy. He acquired an education in the visual arts; as a writer he largely educated himself by wide reading. Friends paid for the publication of his youthful *Poetical Sketches*, but Blake could not find a publisher for *Songs of Innocence and Experience*, written in his thirties. He engraved them himself, cutting the text alongside the illustrations, and he and his wife Catherine Boucher tinted the sheets by hand and bound them into little books of incomparable beauty. Blake was very unusual among men of genius in having married wisely and happily. Such esteem as he won during his lifetime was for his work as an engraver, and he died neglected and in poverty.

In considering his passionate, visionary works both as an artist and a poet, it is natural to recall that he lived on the cusp of the change from the intellectual atmosphere of the Enlightenment to that of Romanticism, and his life span coincided with the early Industrial Revolution, while his early works were published during the outbreak of the French Revolution, of which Blake and the radical circle in which he moved at first fervently approved.

Locating Blake's revolutionary opinions in the ferment of his time will help us appreciate his work, however, only if we also recognize that his vision largely concerns the timeless aspects of the human situation and the problematic interface between human and divine. Blake detested theism and atheism equally. He combined hatred of organized religion:

> The gates of this chapel were shut
> And "Thou shalt not" writ over the door....

with a deeply religious vision in which the whole creation is suffused with the divine and every human desire is sacred, including sexual joy:

Abstinence sows sand all over
The ruddy limbs & flaming hair
But desire gratified
Plants fruits of life & beauty there.

For Blake imagination, not reason, is the supreme human faculty that alone can encompass the infinite. He worked out his vision in long symbolical poems, the "Prophetic Books" full of personified figures in his own invented mythology, wrestling with an inverted version of Christianity in which the natural is holy and the doctrinal and disciplined are devilish. The result is as impenetrable to most readers as a dark night, though shot through with sparks of perception like sporadic stars.

It is in his lyric poetry that Blake's peculiar vision of the world has entered our culture. The *Songs of Innocence and Experience* combine such intensity of thought and feeling with such simplicity of expression that they are incandescent, at once lucid and mysterious, their encapsulated complexity unfolding in the mind for hours, months, and years after one has read them. As for example, "The Tyger," a poem that encompasses the problem of evil:

Did he smile his work to see?
Did he who made the lamb make Thee?

Which is known to every schoolchild, and blazes in the mind of all who read it.

Blake is the poet of the incarnation, for he proclaims a fusion of the divine with the human; he is the poet of immanence, for he saw the divine shining through the material world around him. He is the poet of original sin, measuring the gulf between innocence and experience. He fully obeyed the injunction to become as a little child to enter the kingdom of heaven, yet his indignation at the ills of the world around him, the burden of experience, is as sharp as that of a prophet calling for repentance:

> Is this a holy thing to see
> In a rich and fruitful land
> Babes reduced to misery,
> Fed with cold, and usurous hand?

Like Christ among the Pharisees, he blamed "the mind-forged manacles" of formal doctrine.

Is it possible to separate the perfect fusion he achieved and consider the spiritual content of his work apart from its enduring beauty? His rejection of material explanations of the world and his powerful assertion of the need to see the spiritual beyond the physical seem a more necessary corrective than ever as scientific ideas become the measure of all things.

The atoms of Democritus
And Newton's particles of light
Are sands upon the Red Sea shore
Where Israel's tents do shine so bright.

The beauty of Blake's works gives a sort of self-validating quality to his thought, because his thought was largely about the quality of beauty in the world: "What," it will be questioned, "when the sun rises do you not see a round disc of fire somewhat like a guinea?" "O no, no, I see an innumerable company of the heavenly host crying, 'Holy, holy holy is the Lord God Almighty.'"

"If the doors of perception were cleansed," he said, "everything would appear as it is, infinite."

Reading him is a potent way of cleansing perception.

□

Jill Paton Walsh is the author of Knowledge of Angels.

Seraphim of Sarov
(1759–1833)

by Richard Price

At a conference in St. Petersburg a few years ago, a visiting Italian asked in all innocence why Pushkin, though a contemporary of the most beloved of modern Russian saints, St. Seraphim of Sarov, never visited him and is not known to have taken the slightest interest in him. Her question was received in stunned silence. The fact is too embarrassing for modern Russians in quest of a single national identity: Pushkin and St. Seraphim represent two contrasting cultures that did not know each other and did not wish to know each other.

To find St. Seraphim we have to leave behind the urban, cosmopolitan world of Pushkin and wend our way into the forests of southern Russia, into a monastic culture fed by constant reading from the Bible and the lives of the early saints. For Seraphim the world of the early monks and hermits provided models of sanctity for every age. He himself imitated St. Anthony of Egypt by spending decades in strict seclusion, with virgin forest as his equivalent of the desert; for 1,000 nights and days he imitated St. Symeon the Stylite by standing and praying on a rock. Just as St. Anthony eventually came out of seclusion to act as a spiritual father, so Seraphim, in the last eight years of his life, opened the doors of his cell to whoever wished to consult him.

Visitors made the long journey in prodigious numbers: There could be up to 2,000 of them waiting round his cell. They flocked to him for the same reason that comparable numbers had gone to see Symeon the Stylite a millennium and a half before: They saw in him a man of authority whose years as a recluse made him a privileged visitor from another world, qualified to speak as the mouthpiece of God's love for each individual.

What guidance did Seraphim offer his visitors? As a priest he regularly absolved them from their sins without demanding a detailed confession. His confidence in the power of divine grace led him to affirm that all those united to the Christ through the Eucharist would be saved; he taught strict observance of the rules of the church but refused to turn this into a condition for salvation. The severe asceticism that he himself practiced shows that he did not water down the demands of the faith; but he had a vivid sense of the church as the communion of saints living and dead, whose self-sacrifice atoned for the failings of others. His favorite theme was the joy that radiates from our sense of the power of Christ present to heal and save. His customary greeting to everyone who came to him was, "You my joy, Christ is risen."

As the ideal spiritual father, Seraphim enjoyed a popularity in his lifetime that developed into a cult after his death, akin to those which in the West arose round the Curé of Ars and, more recently, Padre Pio. In him was revived the figure of the *starets* (spiritual father) familiar in Byzantium and old Russia. Nevertheless, Seraphim's canonization in 1903 was forced on a reluctant church hierarchy by Tsar Nicholas II, who wanted a miracleworking saint as a symbol of national revival and as a heavenly patron in the war he was planning against Japan. Seraphim became associated with a body of dubious prophecies, some of them anti-Semitic, and including a supposed assurance that the latter part of Nicholas's reign would be long and glorious. It is to the credit of the Russian hierarchy that it discouraged the circulation of these prophecies, which have never played any part in the popular cult of the saint.

The canonization was accompanied by the publication of the *Conversation with Motovilov,* in which Seraphim reveals at length his teaching on the charisms of the Holy Spirit, leading up to the extraordinary climax where Motovilov sees Seraphim's face shining with a heavenly light, like that of Christ on Mount Tabor. The work had been "discovered" by an unscrupulous propagandist who was simultaneously engaged in the publication of the most notorious of all literary forgeries, the *Protocols of the Elders of Sion.* The *Conversation* has become accepted as one of the classics of Russian spirituality, but it surely reflects the extravagant mysticism of the last tsarist court, with its roots in Western pietism, though some elements in the work derive from the spirituality of Byzantine and Russian monasticism and may be accepted as authentic, notably the stress on the religion of the heart and on spiritual joy.

The Russian devotion to both Seraphim and Pushkin expresses a clasping on to cultural roots and a nostalgia for a supposedly golden age. Both men remain unspoiled by such treatment: They come across as remarkably fresh and independent personalities. The simultaneous devotion of so many Russians to both symbolizes not only the tensions in Russian culture but the paradox of the vitality of Christianity in a post-Christian age.

◻

Richard Price lectures in church history at Heythrop College in the University of London.

Søren Kierkegaard
(1813–1855)

by George Pattison

In the summer of 1835 a twenty-two-year-old theology student, Søren Kierkegaard, spent a holiday at Gilleleie, a fishing village on the northern coast of Denmark. There, on the cliff tops overlooking the transparent azure waters, he reflected on the meaning and direction of his troubled young life. He recalled the succession of family deaths and felt the loneliness of bereavement that seemed to epitomize the human condition. He was pondering a career as an academic theologian, but what good, he asked himself, would be the pursuit of a merely theoretical truth, when what matters "is to find a truth which is truth *for me,* to find the *idea for which I am willing to live and die.*" In the next few years these questions were to be sharpened, as his indecision about his future dragged on, culminating in his breaking off his engagement to Regine Olsen, a girl he deeply loved but realized he could not marry, for complex reasons probably associated with his guilt-ridden relation to his father.

In those summer days of 1835, Kierkegaard effectively staked out the course of his future authorship. Out of a romantic image of poetic melancholy he generated the quintessentially modern archetype of the angst-ridden, alienated outsider, the solitary individual pitted against the infernal machine of the system. In Kierkegaard's day "the system" meant first and foremost the system of Hegelian philosophy, with its grand claims for the all-encompassing reach of science. In a succession of pseudonymous works, he launched a devastating attack on the pretensions of Hegelianism and on the reductive, deterministic view of human life that he saw it leading to. The very titles of such works as *Fear and Trembling, Philosophical Fragments, Concluding Unscientific Postscript*, and *The Concept of Anxiety* convey something of the flavor and nature of the attack. Philosophy could not comprehend the divine paradox of the incarnation, seeing in the assertion that this individual human being was also God an offense against reason. Nor could it throw light on the dark, irrational places of the human soul.

At the same time Kierkegaard came to realize that the romantic melancholy he felt so deeply in himself was another form of nihilism, a refusal to trust that God has made all things for good, and was an evasion of personal responsibility. Simply rejecting science and the claims of social life was to shirk the challenge, not to overcome it. The romantic youth must face up to ethical responsibility and, finally, be confronted by the Christian challenge to his narcissistic cult of self. These were the issues at the heart of his novel-like books *Either/Or, Repetition* and *Stages on Life's Way*.

As Kierkegaard understood it, the reductionism and collectivism of the Hegelians and the self-indulgence of aestheticism were twin symptoms of an intellectual, social, and moral collapse. Only religion and, in the last resort, a radical form of Christian discipleship, could provide a remedy. Now, alongside his pseudonymous works he published under his own name a sequence of increasingly demanding religious meditations. When he felt that what he was propounding went beyond what he himself could live up to, he took on a new pseudonym, under which he published *Training in Christianity* and *The Sickness unto Death*.

Kierkegaard's relation to Denmark's state church was always ambivalent, and finally became openly hostile. He argued that established Christianity necessarily "soft-pedaled" the challenge of what he called "New Testament Christianity." He saw the church as too eager to assimilate its message to the philosophy of the day (whether Hegelianism or Platonism), to blur the truth for the sake of numbers (the three thousand converts on the first Pentecost, he remarked, were a sign of things to come), and, forgetting its essential other-worldliness, to give its blessing to the characteristic forms of this-worldly life: marriage, child-bearing, and the state. Against Luther's insistence on faith alone, Kierkegaard called for a rediscovery of the active imitation of Christ. In 1855, the last year of his life (he died at forty-two), these criticisms came together in a series of pamphlets in which he challenged the clergy to admit that "Christendom" was essentially a compromise with the world.

Kierkegaard declared Christ to be the absolute paradox, and his own life was a succession of paradoxes; he has been claimed by Christian radicals and conservatives alike. His may seem a dark vision, emphasizing absurdity, sin, the cross, and suffering, but he wrote no less emphatically of God's goodness in creation, of grace and of joy in the midst of sufferings if we live—as he put it—with "the expectation of an eternal happiness." Perhaps what is truly Kierkegaardian is that all of these themes are refracted through the reflective spirit of modernity, demonstrating that it is possible both to live from the resources of Christian faith and to be true to our modern—and postmodern—experience and identity.

◻

George Pattison is dean of chapel at King's College, Cambridge.

Thérèse of Lisieux
(1873–1897)

---

by James McCaffrey

"Irritating," "boring," and "almost repulsive" is how Karl Rahner described her, and he is the voice of many. "A sweet little sister who never did anything," said one of her own community. Popular carica-tures and sugary representations do not help either. Her language, some-times soft and sentimental, often cloys. Even her writings were stripped at first by others of every-thing deemed offensive to the pious reader. Yet her admirers are legion, ardent, and diverse, ranging from the Jewish philosopher Henri Bergson, the theologian Hans Urs von Balthasar, and Mother Teresa of Calcutta to Jack Kerouac. For Pope Pius X, she was "the greatest saint of modern times."

Born in 1873, she had to struggle all her life with a difficult temperament. "Thoughtless" and "stubborn" is how her mother described her—a spoiled child, highly sensitive, touchy, moody, and capable of violent outbursts. But she was also made of steel. When only fourteen, she defied Vatican protocol to plead in vain with Leo XIII for permission to enter Carmel, which she later did at fifteen. There she lived, practically unknown, until her death at the age of twenty-four.

Story of a Soul, her autobiography, ranks with the great spiritual classics. Her spirituality is firmly rooted in the ordinary, the messiness and grind of daily living. It already proclaimed the message of the Second Vatican Council that holiness is for everyone. Her superior described her at twenty as "filled with tricks, a mystic, a comedienne." Her God is no stern lawgiver. She gave holiness a new look.

Her French family was tinged with the rigorous Jansenism prevalent in her day. But the church she loved was not a lifeless pyramid of laws and structures. It was a community of sinners constantly in need of mercy, weak and broken strugglers like herself, its "heart burning with love." She could check a misguided superior's abuse of authority with one sentence: "There are some rules which no one has the right to impose." She voiced the hurt of many women in our own day. Her desire to be a priest is well known—"something deeply felt," her sister assures us, "which raised high hopes in her." She is a sure guide to the maternal heart of God.

She is best known for her "little way"—"little" in the gospel sense, a simple path designed for the "little ones," the *anawim*, the poor of Yahweh who trust in his merciful love alone.

"It is to recognize our weakness, to expect everything from God, as a little child expects everything from its father." It took her a lifetime of struggle to live it out fully.

We learn the cost of it for her from her "night of nothingness" during the last eighteen months of her life, when, covered in "thick darkness," she was haunted by "mocking voices," tempted to "suicide" and "blasphemy," and teetered on the brink of despair. With a rare touch of originality she encourages us in our pain "to carry our crosses weakly…suffer weakly and without courage." She doubted, and she questioned, saying, "I no longer believe in eternal life." But she saw it as part of her mission to be one with unbelievers, anguished as they were by the silence of God.

The account of her death reads like the story of the crucifixion. She said, "All I have is love." In our culture that sanctions abortion, euthanasia, and assisted suicide, she reaffirms that life is sacred and love is primary. For her, every kind of pain—rejection, poverty, failure, genocide, discrimination, depression—even death itself—can be transformed into an experience of love, not just endured stoically.

Her deathbed conversation says it all: "You ought to try to sleep," said her sister Celine.

"I cannot. I am praying."
"What are you saying to Jesus?"
"I say nothing….I just love him."

Her constancy in quiet prayer provides today a much needed balance to some more demonstrative modern prayer movements. Her writings are mosaics of biblical texts and anticipate the call of the church to rediscover the scriptures. The Jesus she met in the Gospels was the Word made weakness, her Lover, who was frail and human like herself, and like herself passionately in need of love: "Jesus, my only love." She says it all in a few lines of her poem, "To the Sacred Heart of Jesus":

> I need a heart burning with tenderness,
> To be my support for ever,
> To love everything in me, even my weakness,
> And never to leave me day or night....
> I must have a God who takes on my nature
> And becomes my brother and is able to suffer.

□

James McCaffrey is editor of Mount Carmel, A Review of the Spiritual Life. *He has written extensively on St. Thérèse.*

Fyodor Mikhailovich Dostoevsky
(1821–1881)

by Irina Kirillova

After the fall of the Soviet regime in 1991, Russia moved rapidly into a period of new writing, new music, new theatre. But one nineteenth-century classical writer—Dostoevsky—remains widely read and avidly studied as a source of religiously based, absolute moral values to replace discredited, ideologically defined "Soviet morality." For Dostoevsky, any stable system of values must be rooted in the teaching and the person of Jesus Christ—man and God.

Dostoevsky was born in 1821. His father, a doctor, who gave his son the run of his very progressive medical library, sent him to St. Petersburg to become a military engineer. The young Dostoevsky, however, showed a marked preference for literature and philosophy and had several published works to his name when, in 1847, he joined an illegal "secret society," the Petrashevsky Circle, and within that circle a radical revolutionary core. As he said later, he wanted to know at first hand the men who were dedicated to the idea of total destruction in the name of a future utopia. The utopian idea, particularly in its early-nineteenth-century form of Christian socialism, fascinated Dostoevsky to the end of his life.

This demythologized social Christianity and the suffering of the innocents, particularly children, destroyed the faith in which Dostoevsky had grown up. But even when he rejected the mystical and sacramental life of the church, he kept an almost ecstatic veneration for the person of Christ, the "perfect man," who was "the way, the truth and the life." In a letter from Siberia in 1854, he wrote: "If someone were to prove to me that Christ is outside of the truth, and if it were truly so...I would prefer to remain with Christ, rather than with truth."

In 1849 the leading members of the Petrashevsky Circle, including Dostoevsky, were arrested and condemned to death. Awaiting his turn to face the firing squad, Dostoevsky said to a companion, "We shall be with Christ," words hauntingly reminiscent of Christ's promise to the righteous robber, "Today thou shalt be with me in paradise." The execution Dostoevsky expected was commuted at the last moment to penal servitude and exile in Siberia, but he never forgot the expectation of imminent death and the experience inspired the three passionate speeches against the death penalty in his novel *The Idiot*.

The years in Siberia turned him into the writer and visionary of his mature period. He recovered his faith in the divine mystery and the divinity of Christ among the thieves and the murderers of the penal colony. He was overwhelmed by the intensity of their prayer and confession of sins in Holy Week, by their profound awareness of their crimes as sins. In these brutalized faces Dostoevsky saw the "image and likeness of God."

All Dostoevsky's mature novels are essentially concerned with the one theme: the gift of freedom and will given to man and his tragic abuse of it. With the exception of Prince Myshkin and Alyosha Karamazov, his heroes commit the irreversible crime— murder. The killer, whether he kills directly like Raskolnikov, or through others like Stavrogin, becomes a "man god" who usurps the right which only God has, that of taking life. Only the miracle of an act of grace can save the killer's soul. The high point of *Crime and Punishment* is the reading of the raising of Lazarus, a potential symbolic "prefigurement" of Raskolnikov's return to "living life." But in *The Devils* the psychopathic Stavrogin, a "living corpse," comes not to repentance but to despair and suicide. The redemption of the "Great Sinner" was impossible in literary terms: The novel is concerned with the existential and the psychological, and not with the mystery of the spiritual.

The focal point of Dostoevsky's last great novel, *The Brothers Karamazov*, is the legend of the Grand Inquisitor. The silent figure of Christ is confronted with that of the Inquisitor, who makes a chillingly plausible case for what we recognize as totalitarian socialism, which encompassed for Dostoevsky the ultimate evil—the denial of human freedom and dignity. Christ is accused of expecting too much of humanity, which, provided its physical and material needs are satisfied, will willingly abdicate freedom and will. For Dostoevsky, only in Christ can we find perfect freedom and the creative fulfillment of will.

◻

Irina Kirillova is a former lecturer in Russian studies at the University of Cambridge.

William and Catherine Booth
(1829–1912) WILLIAM
(1829–1890) CATHERINE

by Roy Hattersley

William Booth was the most successful evangelist of the nineteenth century. In an age when traveling preachers counted their conversions—and used their weekly totals to advertise for new work—Booth certainly topped the performance league. And, although he never descended to such commercial practices himself, he took great pride in his unparalleled talent for saving souls. But his importance centered around the world he took as his parish. The poor were his natural congregation and, at least in his early days, the only people who listened to his sermons were the men and women to whom the church would not reach out.

He was right to claim that the Salvation Army was the continuation of John Wesley's work. "We have," he said, with every justification, "gone on, only a great deal further, along the lines he travelled." Wesley had filled the vacuum that had been left, in the eighteenth century, by indolent Church of England clergy. But a hundred years later Wesleyan preachers seemed similarly detached from the hard world of the Industrial Revolution. Booth—who regarded theological speculation as a waste of time—believed that the Methodists concentrated on scholarship at the expense of what he called "practical Christianity." So he deserted the doctors of theology and formed the Army, which met the needs of the neglected masses by advancing into the highways and byways and making potential converts come into its citadels.

Everything Booth did, as the Army gradually evolved from the East London Mission, was geared to the needs and the inclinations of the industrial poor. The bands and the banners were intended to lead them from the streets into church. The uniforms were calculated to appeal to the jingoism of Victorian England as well as making every officer a visible affirmation of belief in the cause and the corps. The reformed sinners who preached on the street corners attracted the attention of the passers-by because they were of the same social class as the men and women at whom their exhortations were directed. William Booth was God's salesman as well as God's soldier. And he had identified his natural market.

The success of his technique was swift and spectacular. Within ten years of the Salvation Army's inauguration, Booth commanded 3,000 corps and 10,000 full-time officers, with outposts as far-flung as Iceland and New Zealand, Argentina and

Germany. But his early preoccupation with the poor was more than a shrewd analysis of how he could best succeed. On his first Christmas Day in London, he realized that the East End unemployed visited the hated public houses because the barrooms offered the only warmth and comfort in their lives. From then on he had no doubt that cold and hunger did the devil's work.

Catherine—the stronger, cleverer, and certainly more attractive partner in the near-perfect Booth marriage—had understood the hard facts of deprivation ever since, walking across wasteland, she had found a bundle of rags which, on closer inspection, turned out to be a woman who had given birth a couple of hours earlier. That incident inspired her lifelong campaign to improve the position of women in nineteenth-century society. Combined with her defense of women's right to preach—supported by irrefutable scriptural evidence—her campaign to raise the age of consent and change the laws on prostitution and procuring made her one of the great social reformers of her age. Because of her, William Booth became a social reformer too.

In the year of Catherine's death, William Booth published *In Darkest England and the Way Out*, the first comprehensive plan for ending poverty in the whole country. His proposals were hopelessly utopian. Their error was overoptimism. He believed that, given the chance, London prostitutes would choose to leave the streets of the capital and take jobs as milkmaids and domestic servants in the country. But optimism is a sign of grace. William Booth believed in redemption.

Because of that, he refused to make a distinction between the deserving and the undeserving poor—at least as far as the amelioration of their misery was concerned. He wanted to redeem the unrighteous. But he would not deny them material help while they were making their slow way to redemption. It was a philosophy that had a profound influence on the opinions of Victorian England and, in itself, made William Booth an important historical figure. It also made him hated by the establishment. By nature he was always on the side of authority. But for most of his life the powerful feared as well as loathed him.

His most obvious claim to a place in the Victorian pantheon is the new church that he created. Yet the untutored pawnbroker's clerk from Nottingham who founded a worldwide movement is rarely accorded the distinction he deserves. That is, in part, because his military postures appeared ridiculous to sophisticated opinion. But his exclusion from the roll of eminent Victorians has a more important cause. William Booth's work was amongst the poor. That work is always undervalued.

□

Roy Hattersley is the author of Blood and Fire: William and Catherine Booth and their Salvation Army.

John Henry Newman
(1801–1890)

by Owen Chadwick

The life of John Henry Newman was marked by two conversions. The first was as a schoolboy, aged fifteen—a Calvinistic evangelical experience. It was a powerful memory. Much later, at the age of forty-two, as his Anglican convictions waned, he resigned his parish of St. Mary's, Oxford, and at his little chapel in the hamlet of Littlemore nearby, preached his last Anglican sermon, "The Parting of Friends," both emotional and moving. After two more years of hesitation he made his decision. When Father Dominic Barberi, the Italian Passionist, came to Littlemore, Newman asked to be received by him into the Church of Rome.

His achievement was profound. He instructed Roman Catholics to rest more easily in their faith. The ultramontane

Catholic world of the nineteenth century was dedicated but narrow. Newman commended a doctrine of development which allowed them to accept that history affects religion and that historical change is inevitable. He pushed them outward intellectually on foundations he built, as regards, for example, the nature of faith. He taught them to be more generous to other denominations, for no Roman Catholic priest before had ever said thank you to the Anglicans with such heartfelt eloquence as Newman in his spiritual autobiography, the *Apologia pro vita sua*.

He had great influence on the Anglicans whom he left. With Keble and Pusey and others, he enabled them to be conscious of their Catholic inheritance—especially with regard to the sacraments, ways of prayer, and the value of religious life.

In 1851 and 1852 he was persuaded to be the first head of a new Catholic university at Dublin. The venture failed because of the Irish bishops, not through any fault of Newman's. But out of it came his lectures on "The Idea of a University," which are still discussed by academic theorists in a wholly different world a century and a half later. His approach was impracticable then and is still more impracticable now, but some of the writing is imperishable for those who care about the culture of humanity.

Beneath the achievements, there was the person. He had a rare sense of himself in front of God: Creator and created, alone to alone. God—present in sacrament, in nature, immediate, transforming, and glorious—was too instant for debate. Newman has wrongly been charged with thinking that reason has nothing to do with faith. But for him, God is simply there. It is not the philosophers but the children, the simple and obedient consciences, who know God. We shall not talk people into finding him. You face God, you do not need to argue.

He felt most deeply for the way conscience is led by the Spirit: "If I am obliged to bring religion into after-dinner toasts (which indeed does not seem quite the thing) I shall drink—to the Pope, if you please—still, to conscience first, and to the Pope afterwards." When young, he read about St. Athanasius, who became a lifelong hero: Here was the lone mind, criticized, even hated, but unflinching in its stand for God's truth in the world.

He founded the Oratory at Birmingham and later its school. When he arrived in Rome as a convert he knew that he should enter a religious order, but which one? When he visited the Oratory, founded by St. Philip Neri in Rome, it seemed to him that he would feel at home in such a community, as formerly when he was a fellow of an Oxford college. It had a tradition of learning, and he was an academic by training. He felt a vocation to the single life and to the way of retirement.

The quiet way was his way: as minister in the Birmingham parish; teaching in school; writing articles for religious periodicals. He came out of seclusion only when he felt the church direly needed him, as when an ex-Dominican told stories of sexual malpractice to damage the Catholic reputation; or when Charles Kingsley, who despite his eminence had a conventional anti-Catholic prejudice, accused Catholic priests of having no sense of truth; or when Gladstone, a former prime minister, was grieved by the First Vatican Council and said that Catholics could not help being disloyal to the state. Newman rose in wrath and destroyed the charges one by one. No one could be more devastating against prejudice. But this public face was not the way of life that he wanted. When Pope Leo XIII made him a cardinal, the fashionable Millais painted his portrait in the ecclesiastical robes. The sitter looks uncomfortable, as though he doubts whether he should be in this situation.

His reflections on the way of faith have ever since gladdened and strengthened the hearts of many. *The Dream of Gerontius* is a poem on a dying soul appearing before its Maker and Judge: again, the soul face to face with its Creator. In it Newman included a hymn that became beloved in many lands: "Praise to the Holiest in the Height." Another of the hymns composed by this lover of music, capable of bold lines, is one of the most prayerful in any language: "Lead, Kindly Light"; verse heartfelt, penitent, humble, full of a sense of movement in the Spirit, which triumphs at last.

□

Owen Chadwick was Dixie Professor of Ecclesiastical History at Cambridge from 1958 to 1968 and Regius Professor of Modern History from 1968 to 1983.

Karl Barth
(1886–1968)

by George Hunsinger

Karl Barth, the Swiss Reformed professor and pastor, was once described by Pope Pius XII as the most important theologian since Thomas Aquinas. His enormous contribution to theology, church, and culture will take generations to assimilate and assess. As the principal author of "The Barmen Declaration," he was the intellectual leader of the German "Confessing Church," the Protestant congregations that resisted Hitler.

Never having studied for a doctorate, Barth, who started out as a village pastor, did more than anyone to revitalize theology in the twentieth century. Among his many books, sermons and essays, the great multivolume *Church*

Dogmatics—a closely reasoned, eloquently stated argument in nearly 10,000 pages—stands out as his crowning achievement. It remained unfinished—like the cathedral in Strasbourg, he once quipped, with its missing tower. Thoroughly modern, he rejected modernism in theology. Deeply traditional, he left no stone of tradition upon another. Without deterring easy classification on the part of critics, he has defied easy classification. Not since Luther and Calvin has there been a Protestant theologian so prodigious in output yet so active in worldly affairs, both ecclesiastical and political. From early years when he was known as the "Red Pastor" for his involvement with organizing workers, to his theological leadership of the Confessing Church during the Third Reich, to his protest against Western prosecution of the "Cold War" and his increasingly antimilitarist, antinuclear stance, he was always a public intellectual embroiled in ceaseless controversy. He believed that theologians should work with a Bible in one hand and a newspaper in the other.

During the last decade of his life, Barth was increasingly hopeful about the "astonishing renewal" in the Catholic Church initiated by the Second Vatican Council. "I often sense in Catholicism," he once said, "a stronger Christian life than in the Protestant churches." After reading Hans Küng's book *Justification* (1957), whose thesis was that the teachings of Barth and Catholicism were compatible, Barth stated: "It occurs to me as something worth pondering that it could suddenly take place that the first will be last and the last first, that suddenly from Rome the doctrine of justification by faith alone will be proclaimed more purely than in most Protestant churches."

Within the Augustinian and Calvinistic traditions he inherited, Barth's doctrine of election was notable for being strongly revisionist. Predestination, Barth proposed, was not God's dreadful decree that determined the eternal destiny of the human race by a separation of the "sheep" from the "goats." On the contrary, grounded in the Holy Trinity, election was God's eternal self-determination not to be God without us, but rather to be God for us in Jesus Christ. The electing God is the God who speaks both a yes and a no—yes to creation; no to sin, evil, and death. In Christ, whose death and resurrection embodied them both for our sakes, the no is overridden by the yes.

This profound revision, perhaps Barth's greatest contribution to the history of doctrine, could not but have ramifications throughout the whole of his theology. The freedom of God was to be answered at every point by responsible human freedom.

Another notable theme in Barth was that doctrine and ethics must not be separated, especially when it came to grave social evils. "It is not enough," he once stated, "only to say, 'Jesus is risen,' but then to remain silent about the Vietnam War." Ethics without doctrine, Barth believed, was nothing, but doctrine without ethics was worse than nothing. In modern Protestant theology, he contended, neither the left nor the right could adequately proclaim the Gospel. Neither knew how to uphold doctrinal substance simultaneously with contemporary relevance. The left wanted relevance without substance, even as the right wanted substance without relevance—the very impasse Barth discerned in the nineteenth century. "These two extremes," he stated, "...are for me a thing of the past. On both sides one must go forward instead of always moving backwards."

Barth was above all a God-intoxicated human being. "Theology," he wrote, "is a peculiarly beautiful discipline. Indeed, we can confidently say that it is the most beautiful of all disciplines. To find academic study distasteful is the mark of the Philistine. It is an extreme form of Philistinism to find, or to be able to find, theology distasteful. The theologian who labours without joy is not a theologian at all. Sulky faces, morose thoughts and boring ways of speaking are intolerable in this field."

Reputed for sharp polemic, Barth's infectious childlike joy, his self-deprecating humor, his love for Mozart, and his profound understanding of Scripture have endeared him to many whose lives he has immeasurably enriched.

□

George Hunsinger is director of the Center for Barth Studies at Princeton Theological Seminary.

Pope John XXIII
(1881–1963)

---

by Richard McBrien

If John XXIII could be called the greatest pope in history, it was a greatness rooted not only in his pastoral achievements but in his personal sanctity. Embodying a rare combination of profound holiness and unparalleled authority, he consistently applied the enormous power of his office to the service of others.

Born Angelo Roncalli, the fourth of thirteen children in a family of peasant farmers, his life's sole desire was to become a holy priest, totally obedient to the will of God (thus his episcopal motto, "Obedience and peace"). Were it not for a chance meeting with Achille Ratti, the librarian at the Ambrosian Library in Milan, where he was doing historical research into the life of St. Charles Borromeo, Angelo Roncalli might never have left his home diocese of Bergamo.

Ratti become pope in 1922, taking the name Pius XI, and launched Roncalli on a diplomatic career in the church that would take him to Bulgaria, Turkey, and Greece, where he saved thousands of Jews from deportation and death, then to France as nuncio, and finally to Venice as its cardinal-archbishop. Toward the end of his life, Roncalli acknowledged that these years in the East and in France had given him the cultural and religious breadth to transcend the limits of his peasant background.

When he was elected to the papacy on 28 October 1958, less than a month shy of his seventy-seventh birthday, it was generally expected that he would be a so-called transitional pope, following one of the longest pontificates in history, that of Pius XII. But he proved the pundits wrong.

At his coronation Mass in St. Peter's Basilica on 4 November, the feast of St. Charles Borromeo, the senior cardinal-deacon, in keeping with a millennium-long custom, placed an imperial tiara on the new pope's head, while reciting the ancient formula: "Know that you are the father of princes and kings, pontiff of the whole world and Vicar of Christ on earth." Given the extraordinarily humble and self-effacing persona that John XXIII would almost immediately disclose to the world, that whole scene, in retrospect, could not have been more incongruous.

From the outset, he signaled that he would be a very different kind of pope: a servant rather than a sovereign, a pastor rather than a patrician, a priest rather than a prelate. He sounded the keynote for his pontificate in the homily of the Mass that, contrary to tradition, he delivered himself. He would not be "the father of princes and kings," but a good shepherd, after the pattern of Jesus himself.

On his first Christmas as pope, he revived the custom of visiting the sick, including a hospital for children. On the next day he went to Regina Coeli Prison, where he recalled the jailing of one of his own relatives. "You could not come to visit me," he told the prisoners, "so I came to see you!" Thereafter, he made frequent appearances at local parishes, convalescent homes for the elderly, hospitals, schools, and charitable institutions. On Holy Thursday, the following spring, he revived the custom of washing the feet of selected members of the congregation, and on Good Friday he walked in the procession of the cross. More than any other pope since the earliest centuries, he recognized that he was, before all else, a pastor, the bishop of Rome.

John XXIII's greatest single achievement, to be sure, was his launching of the Second Vatican Council in 1962. Although convinced that the church needed an *aggiornamento* ("updating"), as he called it, its details did not begin to take shape in his mind until his celebrated opening speech to the council on 11 October 1962. It would be a council not to censure and condemn heretics and dissenters, but to promote human solidarity through the spreading of "the fullness of Christian charity." He and his council together launched a recovery of Catholic humanism.

John showed himself to be as shrewd and politically astute a leader as he was a kind and gentle pastor. He shaped the direction of the council by intervening at crucial points in the first session, spoke out effectively during the Cuban missile crisis, affording the Soviet premier Nikita Krushchev a face-saving opportunity to withdraw, and later issued his "last will and testament" in his bold and forward-looking encyclical *Pacem in Terris* (Peace on Earth).

Before the end of the year, however, he was diagnosed as having terminal stomach cancer. As he lay dying in his papal apartment several months later, the media provided a continual flow of messages from his deathbed—prayers for various segments of the human community, especially those who, like himself, were afflicted with sickness and suffering. When word of his death flashed around the globe on 3 June 1963, the world found itself bound together in unprecedented solidarity—of the sort that he himself had sought to promote. In a century marked by so much oppression and violence against humanity, Pope John XXIII stood out as a luminous embodiment of warmth, tolerance, inclusiveness, gentleness, humility, patience, and simple, unadorned love—the marks, indeed, of a saint.

A few months after his death, an English-language tour group, led by an Italian guide, paused briefly at his tomb in the crypt of St Peter's. Speaking in heavily accented English, she pointed it out to her charges as "the tomb of Pope John XXIII, the most beloved pope in all of history."

□

Richard McBrien is the Crowley-O'Brien-Walter Professor of Theology at the University of Notre Dame.

Swami Abhishiktananda
(1910–1973)

---

by Michael Barnes

If the Second Vatican Council marked the beginning of what Karl Rahner called a genuine "world church," then one of its most effec‑ tive apostles was a French monk called Henri le Saux. Better known by his Indian name, Swami Abhishiktananda (literally "bliss of the anointed one"), le Saux will be remembered as a patron saint of interfaith dialogue. He sought to immerse himself totally in the spiritual world of Hinduism while remaining faithful, sometimes at enormous personal cost, to Christ and his church.

He was born in 1910 into a conventionally devout Catholic family at St. Briac in Brittany and became a Benedictine monk at the age of nineteen. In 1950 he realized a dream to go to India where, with a diocesan priest from Lyons called Jules Monchanin, he founded the Shantivanam ashram in Tamil Nadu, South India. He was thus the predecessor of another remarkable European missionary-monk, Bede Griffiths, who made Shantivanam, the "grove of peace," the most famous interfaith pilgrimage center in the world.

But to use the term "missionary" of these "saints of Shantivanam" is misleading. None of them wanted to be a missionary in the conventional sense. They went to India, each in his different way, convinced that God was calling them to a life of contemplative prayer at the heart of a profoundly religious culture.

Monchanin, a brilliant theologian and a close friend of Henri de Lubac, died in 1957 and never saw his hopes for a church transformed by the spirit of India realized. Bede Griffiths moved to Shantivanam in 1968, just as the reforms of the Second Vatican Council were beginning to bear fruit. Some years earlier Abhishiktananda had begun a life of seclusion in the Himalayas, where he lived until a sudden heart attack in December 1973. There is something to be said for regarding Monchanin as the "winter of Shantivanam," Abhishiktananda as its "spring," and Bede as its "summer." The image fits Abhishiktananda well. If Monchanin was remarkable for an austere theological wisdom and Bede famous for the warmth of his hospitality, Abhishiktananda was an energetic explorer who committed himself to an ever deeper engagement with the riches of classical Hinduism.

The seminal event in his life was a meeting with a Hindu holy man, Ramana Maharshi, soon after he arrived in India. He was struck by Ramana's holiness and by the fact, he said, that there was "not a spark of Christianity in him." Here was Abhishiktananda's all-dominating experience of the utter mysteriousness of the God whom no language could exhaust. The influence of Ramana stayed with him all his life.

His legacy is twofold. He is a key figure in the history of the postconciliar Catholic Church in India. Even before the Second Vatican Council, Monchanin and Abhishiktananda had introduced many aspects of Indian culture and practice into their daily living and prayer in the ashram. They took the use of Indian scriptures in Christian worship for granted. But, like Monchanin, Abhishiktananda insisted that prayer had to be combined with study. Unceasing in his encouragement of a properly Indian theology and spirituality, he also kept up an enormous correspondence which, thanks to the efforts of friends like Raimon Panikkar and James Stuart, tells the story of a life of constant effort to understand the ways of the unknown God in his adopted land.

But he will be best remembered for the power, if not the clarity, of his writing. Innumerable books and articles bear witness to his passion to explore "the privileged mission" that, he was convinced, India had received from God. At one point he argues that the biblical "mystery of darkness and silence which Jesus has revealed to us as the bosom of the Father" and the upanishadic symbolism of the "untouched, undivided Brahman" discovered in the "cave of the heart" are set together as "the very same mystery." Monchanin wrote with scrupulous awareness of the limits of theology; Abhishiktananda, on the other hand, oscillates in a sometimes violent way between different ideas and concepts, with little attempt to explain their problematic relationship.

Consistency is not his strong point. But, unlike the agonized Monchanin, his aim was never to produce the polished treatise. His experience of Ramana Maharshi taught him how to surrender himself totally to the God whom he recognized as much in the Bible as in the ancient hymns of the Vedic seers or *rishis*. The conviction he wanted to express is that Hinduism and Christianity will only meet where one experiences *moksa*, the inner awakening described in the Upanishads.

Perhaps his finest work is a tiny book called simply *Prayer*. It begins with the scriptural tradition, with Jesus' own prayer to the Father, and with a constant insistence that "praying is simply believing that we are living in the mystery of God." It ends, after a wonderful but never overwhelming dialogue with yogic techniques, upanishadic texts, *bhakti* devotionalism, and the mystery of the OM, the Hindu sacred mantra, by referring everything to the secret of the Trinity. "ABBA is the mystery of the Son," he says, "OM the mystery of the Spirit. But ultimately there is no name for the Father, for the Father can never be known in himself. He is known only through his self-manifestation in the Son and in the Holy Spirit. The Father is that last or fourth part of the OM, which is pure Silence."

□

Michael Barnes is a Jesuit priest who teaches theology of religions at Heythrop College in the University of London.

Charles de Foucauld
(1858–1916)

---

by Ian Latham and Pam Ware

Charles de Foucauld wished to be everybody's brother and friend. In the Sahara, he sought out Muslims and others, not to preach to them but to be with them as a presence of Jesus. He dreamt of small communities of little brothers and little sisters who would live like "Jesus at Nazareth," contemplating Jesus as he imagined Mary and Joseph doing, poor workers like their neighbors.

No one ever joined him. The one companion he nearly attracted to the Sahara was Louis Massignon—who hesitated and married instead.

Born in Strasbourg in 1858, Charles was an orphan and a French aristocrat. Losing all faith at fifteen, he chose to enter the army, searched for happiness in wild extravagance, saw service in

Algeria, and explored Morocco in disguise at the risk of his life. There, the piety of the Muslims drove him back to his own faith. Their reverence for the Koran led him from that holy book to the Gospels. On his return to France he began to seek God. His prayer was answered, and he was "seized" by his "Beloved Brother and Lord Jesus." The treasure was found, but it took the rest of his life to explore its contents.

He gave up his wealth, his first-class ticket through life, to become like Jesus. His penitential asceticism was heroic, though he hid it when he could. For a time he became a Trappist monk. As such, he learned the discipline of prayer in community and found time and space to reflect. Who was this "Jesus"? The human embodiment of God's love ("Our religion is all love"), Jesus was the "man of Nazareth," the "carpenter, the son of Mary," the "poor man…one of us." In fact, meditated Charles, Jesus is, quite simply, "God, the workman of Nazareth." The thirty years of Jesus' life in Nazareth and his lifelong identity as the "Nazarene" struck Charles with ever-increasing force.

This was his discovery: that God has chosen to become involved with his people, not as the rich one, but as the poor one, the one without name or status ("Can anything good come out of Nazareth?").

But where is this Jesus? Charles as a Trappist in Syria was sent to visit a poor Armenian family: He saw there, suddenly, the living image of Jesus' family life and social situation. Now he asked to leave the Trappists and went physically to Nazareth, where he lived as an odd-job man with the Poor Clares.

At the age of forty-three, Charles de Foucauld felt called to begin a mission for the people of the Sahara. Having asked soldier friends for help, he settled near the border of Morocco, at Beni Abbés, a garrisoned oasis. There he had built a small mud and palm building, comprising a chapel with a sand floor, a few tiny cells, and a courtyard. It was to be a place of "adoration" and of "hospitality." He called it the *Khaoua*, "the Fraternity," and writes: "Pray God that I may truly be a universal brother, a brother to each and all in this part of the country, be they Christian, Muslim, Jew or pagan." Here he welcomed sixty to a hundred visitors a day: slaves, poor laborers, soldiers, travelers. People's needs drove him to it. He was hard-pressed to find a quiet time for Mass and his habitual long prayer. Children loved to joke with him. In honor of his radiant, gap-toothed smile, they named a local jagged mountain after him as the "Marabout's Jaw" (*marabout* means "holy man").

He loved the vast silence of the desert, and he had the temperament to persist there, but it was the people who drew him. He was known for his friendship and welcome, for his generosity and trustworthy justice. That was why he was accepted by the Tuareg nomads at Tamanrasset. Here he found a place where he could rest, no longer driven to move on by his inner search for "Nazareth." Most of his work at Tamanrasset was linguistic and anthropological—recording Tuareg diction-aries, stories, culture—but he was grounded in simple friend-ship and good neighborliness—especially after the Tuareg saved his life when he was ill. There he achieved a genuine mutuality.

War broke out in Europe, and in the Sahara rebellion against the French colonialists began. Charles refused to abandon his Tuareg neighbors in spite of the known and obvious danger. He was assassinated on 1 December 1916. After his death, a local chief wrote to his sister: "Charles the Marabout, our friend, has died not only for all of you, he has died for us, too. May God have mercy on him, and may we meet in Paradise."

His legacy is today lived by small groups of laypeople, by fraternities of diocesan priests, and by various religious communities, including the Little Brothers and Little Sisters of Jesus, who share the life of the poorest of people in far-flung corners of the world. For those whose lives have nothing to show, the hope of Jesus' promise holds true: a grain, when it dies, bears fruit.

□

Ian Latham, a member of the Little Brothers of Jesus, lives in community in Peckham, south London. Pam Ware works for the social justice desk of the Conference of Religious in England and Wales.

Edith Stein
(1891–1942)

by Eugene Fisher

Sister Teresa Benedicta of the Cross, Edith Stein, was born a Jew in 1891 in Breslau. She died a Jew in 1942, one of six million of her people systematically rounded up and murdered by the Nazis. For twenty years of her too short life, from 1922 until her death in Auschwitz in 1942, Edith Stein was a devout Catholic, for the last ten years a Carmelite nun. Stein is the only Catholic patron saint of Europe from the twentieth century, the bloodiest in human history, symbolic therefore of the century's highest aspirations and the spiritual resistance to its profound eruptions of evil. Stein said to her sister, Rosa, when they were taken by the Nazis from the convent in Holland where they had sought refuge after fleeing Germany, "Come, we are going for our people." These last recorded words of the saint have been read in various ways, but what cannot be gainsaid is that they bespeak an abiding love for her people, the Jews, and a humble awareness that she was about to die among the people she loved.

Stein could also one day be deservedly made one of the very few women given the title doctor of the church. Her philosophical works, following those of her mentor, Edmund Husserl, were widely translated and influential throughout Europe during her lifetime, as were her later theological works, which employed modern "personalist" philosophical categories. Ironically, because she was a Jew in prewar Germany, she was never able to gain a university position equal to her talents. But this did not stop her from writing, publishing, and lecturing widely.

One of those who studied her works, both as a seminarian in Poland during the Nazi occupation and later as a professor of philosophy himself, was the young Karol Wojtyla, later to become Pope John Paul II. Stein may well come to be seen in the centuries ahead as one of a handful of pivotal Catholic thinkers in the church's history. Certainly, the enterprise of bonding together faith and reason in response to modernity has been one of a very short list of such attempts over the centuries, the first being the patristic era, the second being the great medieval synthesis epitomized by Aquinas. The twentieth century, I would argue, saw the third such moment. And Edith Stein was at the center of it (along, of course, with numerous others).

Stein was raised as an Orthodox Jew. Her book *Life in a Jewish Family*, which she wrote to counter the increasingly anti-

Semitic climate of the Germany of the 1930s, shows her continuing loving respect for the tradition in which she was raised, even after her conversion to Catholicism. But by the time of her conversion, Stein had been a convinced atheist for some years, reflective of her experience in the university. What brought her back to faith in God was the way in which the devout Catholic family of a friend dealt with their loss of a loved one. At their home in their time of grief, she happened to see a copy of the autobiographical *Life* of St. Teresa of Avila. "I began to read," she wrote, "and was immediately caught up and did not stop until the end. When I closed the book, I said to myself: This is the truth."

Edith Stein, both before and after her conversion to Catholicism, was a feminist. She wrote strongly in favor of the equality of men and women before the law and in the marketplace, but held to a theology of "complementarity" between the sexes, acknowledging and, indeed, reveling in the differences between their natures and roles in human destiny. She argued for the ordination of women to the priesthood but rejected the notion that equality meant sameness.

The Jewish community has quite understandably registered concern about the Catholic Church canonizing as a saint a Jewish convert to Catholicism, so rare an event that I, personally, know of no precedent. Did this mean an attempt by Catholics to "coopt" the Holocaust by making it a Catholic rather than a Jewish event? Did it mean to convey to Catholics that the only good Jew is a converted Jew and that an organized missionary effort might be launched by the world's one billion Catholics against the world's fifteen million Jews? The answer to both questions, of course, is a resounding "No!" Catholicism affirms and supports religious liberty and respects Jewish faith as a response to divine revelation. Edith Stein's conversion was a precious, individual event.

On her way to Auschwitz and death, she wrote a last communication to her prioress. "Dear Mother, I am content with everything," she began. Then, referring to the book she had been writing, *The Science of the Cross*, she went on: "One cannot gain a *scientia crucis* unless one is made to feel the cross to the depth of one's being. From the first moment I have been convinced of this and I have said: *'Ave crux, spes unica!'* 'Hail cross, our only hope!'"

□

Eugene Fisher is associate director of the secretariat for ecumenical and interreligious affairs of the U.S. Catholic Bishops' Conference.

Dorothy Day
(1897–1980)

by Robert Ellsberg

In her autobiography, *The Long Loneliness,* Dorothy Day described her first childhood encounter with the lives of the saints. She recalls how her heart was stirred by the stories of their charity toward the sick, the maimed, the leper. "But there was another question in my mind," she notes. "Why was so much done in remedying the evil instead of avoiding it in the first place?...Where were the saints to try to change the social order, not just to minister to the slaves, but to do away with slavery?"

In effect, Day's vocation took form around this challenge. Her conversion to Catholicism and her work in founding the Catholic Worker movement would come many years later. But the great underlying task of her life was to join what Péguy called "the mystical and the political." Long before liberation theology spoke of an option for the poor, Day sensed that it was not enough to feed the poor. Christian faith demanded effective solidarity with the oppressed and a commitment to stand against the structures responsible for so much misery.

There are other Christian prophets whose faith impelled them to radical action. In the case of Day, it was her love of the poor and her passion for social justice that came first, only later leading her to the church. This was an unusual path of conversion in the 1920s, a time when the church was widely regarded as a bulwark of conservatism. She spent her youth working on various radical journals in New York City. Her friends were Communists, anarchists, and other cultural rebels. Nevertheless there was always in Dorothy Day a yearning for the transcendent that distinguished her from her companions. One of them later said that she was too "religious" to make a Communist. As she herself later reflected, borrowing words from a character of Dostoevsky, "All my life I have been haunted by God."

It was an unexpected pregnancy that marked the great turning point in her life. Some years before, at the end of an unhappy love affair, she had had an abortion. Though she never publicly spoke of this event, her evident remorse goes far to explain why, later, while living on Staten Island with a man she deeply loved, the discovery that she was once again pregnant struck such a note of grace. She felt a gratitude so large that it could only be addressed to God. Before long she found herself wishing to have her child baptized in the Catholic Church, a step she soon followed, though it meant a wrenching separation from her common-law husband. It also seemed, initially, to involve a painful betrayal of the workers and the cause of social justice. For five years she waited in the desert, longing to find some way of reconciling her faith and her commitment to the poor, a synthesis, as she put it, "reconciling body and soul, this world and the next."

The answer came with her introduction to Peter Maurin, an itinerant French peasant philosopher. With his inspiration in 1933 she launched the *Catholic Worker*, at first a newspaper and eventually a movement, dedicated to living out the radical social implications of the Gospel. She and the Catholic Workers lived out their faith in voluntary poverty and community among the down-and-out, practicing the works of mercy but also bearing witness against a system that regarded property rather than persons as the measure of value.

Set against the crying needs of the Great Depression, her witness at first attracted enthusiastic support. Some saw the *Catholic Worker* as a Catholic answer to Communism. But later, as her true radicalism and her pacifist convictions became apparent, she was relegated to the prophetic margin of the church. There she remained for much of her life—quietly serving the poor, periodically going to jail for her protests against war and injustice— until the late 1960s, when her uncompromising brand of peacemaking began to find an audience. By the time of her death in 1980, at the age of eighty-three, she was widely regarded as the conscience of the American Catholic Church.

Throughout her life many people irritated Day by calling her a saint. "When they call you a saint," she said, "it means basically that you are not to be taken seriously." But now the American bishops, responding to widespread support, have introduced her cause in Rome. Some feel that it has taken this long to come to grips with the central paradox of her life—her ability to integrate a very traditional style of Catholic piety with a radical style of social engagement. It was a combination that confounded both conservative and liberal admirers.

There was no paradox in her eyes. Her faith and practice were equally rooted in the radical implications of the incarnation—the fact that God had entered our flesh and our history, and so what we did for our neighbors we did directly for him. By the same token she saw no contradiction between loving the church and suffering over its sins and failings. At a time of great polarization in the church, her example in this respect may be one of her greatest gifts. Ultimately, like all the great saints, she devised her own form of holiness, attuned both to the Gospel and the particular challenges of her time.

◻

Robert Ellsberg is the editor of Dorothy Day: Selected Writings.

Simone Weil
(1909–1943)

by David McLellan

Simone Weil, the French philosopher and mystic, has been called "patron saint of all outsiders." Indeed, she resolutely remained outside the Christian church, despite a series of vivid conversion experiences. And her reservations about Christianity itself, since they spring from a deep love for, and adherence to, the Christian Gospel, are among the most challenging of any thinker.

From her birth in Paris in 1909 to her lonely death in a sanatorium in Ashford, Kent, in 1943, Simone Weil lived only thirty-four years. She had published only a few articles and was known only to a small circle of friends. Yet some consider her the greatest spiritual thinker that the West as produced in the past century. At the same time, some have found her off-putting, even repugnant. Certainly there are few lives that involve as much paradox as hers: Born into a comfortable bourgeois family, she became a fanatical supporter of the proletariat; a pacifist, she fought in the Spanish Civil War; a Jew attracted to Christianity, she refused to join the church because of its adherence to the Old Testament. She wrote much—and beautifully—about love, but abhorred all physical contact with her fellows; her outlook on life and politics was somber, even pessimistic, yet she was ever ready to propagate utopian schemes for the reformation of society. Finally, she abjured her splendid gifts by refusing existence itself, and her death was caused, at least partially, by self-starvation, an act of solidarity with her fellow citizens in occupied France.

Simone Weil was one of the cleverest students of her generation. Simone de Beauvoir, Jean-Paul Sartre, Claude Levi-Strauss were her contemporaries and her equals. Like them, she became a philosophy teacher in the *lycée*. Unlike them, and taking literally the ideas of justice and equality with which she had been brought up, she became passionately involved in politics and spent a year working in the Renault factory in Paris. Upon the outbreak of war, she was deprived of her teaching post by the anti-Semitic laws of the Vichy government. Eager to join the Free French Forces in London, she moved south with her parents to Marseilles, en route to North Africa, America, and England. It was in Marseilles that she composed her famous *Notebooks* that were to become the basis of her subsequent reputation. Her thinking was tentative and open-ended, enquiring, probing, and therefore the very opposite of systematic. She particularly aimed to link her conception of Christianity, which was concerned more with the crucifixion than with the resurrection, with two (at first sight) very different traditions: the rich matrix of Mediterranean spirituality, whose centerpieces were Pythagorean thought and Greek philosophy, particularly Plato; and the Hindu emphasis on the *im*personal nature of the divine, and its preference for the idea of balance over that of progress.

In the summer of 1942, Simone Weil at last got her passage to New York. Six months later, she recrossed the Atlantic to join the Free French in London. In the few months left to her, she composed a work entitled *The Need for Roots*, which represents the summation of her thought, recapitulating her favorite themes: her biting criticism of the view of history as progress; her antipathy to Rome and Israel for their sense of special destiny and use of brute force; her admiration for the Greeks; the mistaken dominance given to science in contemporary society; her strong connection of art and literature with moral values; the centrality accorded to physical labor; her unwillingness to consider political institutions, however democratic, as the main legitimizers of the distribution of power; her awareness of the danger of all collective activity; and her insistence that genuine liberty and equality could only be founded by reference to other-worldly values. As she herself remarked: to be always relevant, you have to say things that are eternal.

Throughout her uprooted life Simone Weil did indeed remain an uncompromising outsider, refusing to submit her individuality to any collective authority. The center of her thought, as of her life, was her continual search for the absolute and her continual disappointment. But it is this very restless dissatisfaction that produces the fragmentary brilliance of her writings, which illuminate so many areas of the human condition. For her, contemplation was not a means of stopping a nauseating world and getting off, but of seeing the world in a different and truer perspective, and, above all, of developing a sharp eye and ear for the traces of God in all human activity and experience.

Her trenchant judgments, with their strong individualism and profound sympathy with the outcast, have managed to alienate both left and right and most orthodox religion. But whether we think of her as a twentieth-century saint or condemn her as a self-absorbed dreamer, few can refuse to recognize the challenge her life poses to so many of our own preconceptions, and the unerring instinct with which she managed to go straight to the heart of the problems of our time.

□

David McLellan is visiting professor of political theory at Goldsmith's College, London, and author of Simone Weil: Utopian Pessimist.

Dietrich Bonhoeffer
(1906–1945)

by Edwin Robertson

"I have hardly ever seen a man die so submissive to the will of God," wrote an SS doctor of the last moments of Pastor Dietrich Bonhoeffer, hanged in 1945 for taking part in the bomb plot against Hitler. His last recorded words were for his friend Bishop George Bell of Chichester: "This is the end...but for me the beginning of life."

The daring concepts contained in the letters Bonhoeffer wrote during his last two years in prison have profoundly influenced theology in the West and the Third World. He was a brilliant theologian at an early age. But he turned away from academic work to devote his life to pastoral work in the Church of the Old Prussian Union.

During his studies he met a friendly Catholic priest who offered to guide him through the liturgy of Holy Week in the various churches of Rome. He never forgot this overwhelming spiritual experience. It began a process in his spiritual life which led him safely through the jungle of theological debate that he experienced in his later studies in Berlin and New York.

He had opposed the Nazis from the beginning. Two days after Hitler came to power in 1933, he attacked the leadership principle in a broadcast that was cut off. Several months later he circulated a pamphlet condemning the Nazi treatment of the Jews and refuting the authorities' recourse to Luther's anti-Semitism in an attempt to justify their actions.

He escaped imprisonment by accepting the charge of two German-speaking congregations in London. While there he enabled the world church to know what was really going on in Germany. Through Bishop Bell, then chairman of the World Alliance that later became the World Council of Churches, he brought the ecumenical movement behind those in Germany who resisted the Nazi interference with the church.

In 1939 he refused the safety of an invitation to lecture in America and returned to Germany, where he was forbidden to preach, publish, or hold assembly. Bonhoeffer clearly stated his reasons for going back in a letter to the German Lutheran theologian Reinhold Niebuhr in New York. "Christians in Germany," Bonhoeffer told him, "will face the terrible alternative of either willing the defeat of their nation in order that Christian civilisation may survive or willing the victory of their nation and thereby destroying our civilisation. I know which of these alternatives I must choose, but I cannot make that choice in security."

On his return to Germany, he led an illegal seminary of young theologians who were destined to be leaders in the parishes against the Nazi perversion of the Christian faith. They met at first in a Bible school on the beaches of the Baltic, then at Finkenwalde near Stettin, which was more satisfactory though the conditions there were also primitive. The seminary was eventually closed by the Gestapo.

At the Benedictine monastery at Ettal in Bavaria, Bonhoeffer worked at drafting a new range of ethical attitudes. His writings, particularly *The Cost of Discipleship,* sought to work out a renewed ethical approach in a world dominated by a dimension of evil that had come with the dictators. His most important writing was an unfinished book that is published in England simply as *Ethics.* Here he honors but challenges the old systems of Christian civilization and seeks to reconstruct, instead, a method of "being conformed with Christ."

He then joined the conspiracy against the Nazi regime, meeting the Bishop of Chichester in neutral Sweden to discuss the overthrow and possibly the assassination of Hitler and the conclusion of peace terms with the British. It was an extraordinary step for a Lutheran minister to take. He even talked of sacrificing his righteousness. He was arrested and spent the last two years of his life in prison before he was executed on 9 April 1945. Shortly before his arrest he had become engaged to Maria von Wedermeyer. She marked out with chalk an enclosure the size of his cell on her bedroom floor, so that she could write to him as though she were with him.

The letters he wrote to his friend Eberhard Bethge in those final two years were published in English translation as *Letters and Papers from Prison*. He speculated on the possibility of a "religionless Christianity," out of his disgust with his own church for failing to oppose the evils of National Socialism. He accused its leaders of being concerned only with the preservation of the church "as though that were an end in itself." He wrote of mankind "come of age," and of the need for a "secular holiness."

He saw that the betrayal of the faith in Germany had made the church incapable for the moment of proclaiming the great words of redemption and salvation. Meanwhile activities must be confined to prayer and righteous action. But he believed the time would come when "men will once again be called so to utter the Word of God that the world will be changed and renewed by it. It will be a new language, perhaps quite non-religious but liberating and redeeming...it will be the language of a new righteousness and truth."

What exactly did he mean by this "religionless Christianity"? Perhaps he himself did not quite know. But in more than fifty years we have been unable to shake ourselves free from this man and the questions he posed.

□

Edwin Robertson is the minister at Heath Street Baptist Church, Hampstead, London. He has written extensively on Dietrich Bonhoeffer.

Mother Teresa of Calcutta
(1910–1997)

by Kathryn Spink

Mother Teresa dedicated her life to responding to the Christ who in St. Matthew's Gospel (25:35–45) identified himself with the least of his brothers: those hungry not just for bread but also for love, those naked for want not just of clothes but of compassion, homeless not just because they lacked shelter but because "they had no one to call their own."

Born in Skopje of Albanian parents, by the age of twelve Agnes Bojaxhiu felt called to be a missionary. In 1946, after eighteen years of teaching as a Loreto Sister in India, a "call within a call" crystalized that vocation into a commitment to serve Christ in the "poorest of the poor" while living among them. The objective of the congregation she subsequently founded was to "quench the thirst of Christ on the cross for love and souls."

Controversially, particularly to Western minds, precisely because the dying rescued from the gutters were the crucified Christ, what mattered most was not healing but compassion. If a cure could be effected by a congregation committed to poverty, all the better, but the priority was for the marginalized to die with dignity and not without experiencing the "warmth of a loving hand." Similarly, to Mother Teresa it was inconceivable that the unborn infant Christ should be aborted. She encouraged her Sisters to teach "holy family planning" but, ever a loyal daughter of the church, remained outspokenly opposed to artificial birth control.

With the mission's extraordinarily rapid expansion to over 130 countries, awareness of the spiritual poverty of the materially rich West underlined the need not so much for funds as for the "works of love," which she saw also as "works of peace." God's presence in each individual imposed an immediate responsibility: "Today God gives you and me to be his love and compassion." Perceived by some to lack moral discrimination in pursuit of that end, she believed that because everyone contained the divine life and therefore the potential for goodness, everyone—princess or pauper, dictator, tyrant, or refugee—should be given the opportunity to do good. The call to change political structures or seek justice, though recognized as valid, was not hers. Hers was to deal, one by one, with those whose horizons had shrunk to the bowl of rice they craved. Nor was it for her to judge those who helped provide that rice. Mother Teresa wanted the rich to save the poor and the poor to save the rich. Their mutual salvation depended on the rich giving not from their abundance but "until it hurt." Those seeking to understand were put to work because "love was best proved in deeds" but also because in order to understand poverty you had to "touch" it, you had to touch the body of Christ.

For her sanctity was a "simple duty" for everyone. Yet being a saint meant "I will despoil myself of *all* that is not God." So rigorous was the commitment to being one with, and hence accessible to, the poor that each of her Sisters possessed little more than a bucket and a spare sari. Even when old and suffering from a failing heart, she cheerfully rejected all comforts. "Let the poor eat you up" was her exacting directive, but the requirement was not to do great things but only "small things with great love" and to seek, joyfully, that openness of heart that allowed God to work through his imperfect instruments. She herself was "only the little pencil in God's hand." Her "secret" was prayer. Often she entered a chapel exhausted and emerged shortly afterward, revitalized and totally obedient to whatever, it seemed to her, the Holy Spirit ordained. The energy of God was hers.

"God makes himself the hungry one so that we can satisfy his hunger for our love and he makes himself the Bread of Life that we may eat and live and love." Here is her central vision: Christ crying out for love in the broken bodies of the poor and simultaneously offering himself as sustenance. For her, rooted in an unfaltering, simple faith, knowledge of God was not to be sought through clear images and thought: Hers is an understanding of the heart, that place of direct knowledge. "Do not trust those who come to you with dazzling words about liberty and renovation"—intellectually unsophisticated, the theology she expressed remained essentially that of her pre–Second Vatican Council upbringing in the former Yugoslavia, just as her exhortations to women to be home-makers and leave men to do "what they do best" are an unmodified echo of her mother's attitudes.

Sometimes considered to speak on matters outside her charism and often verbally uncompromising, her profound respect for the manner in which God was at work in every soul resulted, nevertheless, in extreme tolerance. In her presence the medium became the real message and Hindus, Christians, and atheists alike were left in no doubt of the primacy she afforded love. She herself turned the other cheek in response to this world's judgments. "Ye shall know them by their fruits" was the biblical text on which she rested her case.

□

Kathryn Spink is the official biographer of Brother Roger of Taizé, Jean Vanier, Little Sister Magdeleine of Jesus, and Mother Teresa. She was associated with Mother Teresa's work for seventeen years.

Oscar Arnulfo Romero
(1917–1980)

---

by Michael Campbell-Johnston

"Monseñor Romero is an example of life and faith for all Christians and the whole world," declared the present archbishop of San Salvador, Sáenz Lacalle, on the twentieth anniversary of Romero's martyrdom. "San Romero de América," wrote Bishop Casaldáliga in his famous poem shortly after the assassination. The people canonized Romero immediately, though Rome still has to add its official verdict. Romero was shot on the evening of 24 March 1980 while offering Mass in the small chapel of the Divine Providence Hospital, where he lived, just a day after he had made a strong appeal to the ranks in the army and police forces to listen to their consciences and stop obeying immoral commands from their officers to torture and kill fellow Salvadoreans.

Perhaps the most astonishing thing is that none of this was foreseeable. Who could have predicted that, in three short years as archbishop of San Salvador, he would emerge from a timid, retiring conservative figure to become the conscience of a nation, a prophet? When he was first appointed, there was widespread dismay among the more progressive sectors of the church, including his predecessor, Chávez y González. With present hindsight one can only exclaim, *Felix culpa!* There cannot be many examples in church history of high authorities being so mistaken.

What changed Oscar Romero? At the age of sixty, after thirty-five years as a priest and seven as a bishop, what moved him to alter direction so drastically? Some spoke of a "conversion," though Romero himself preferred speaking of rediscovering his roots, the humble life of a peasant family in a rural backwater. Some claim that Romero went to school again. But his teachers were neither university professors nor professional theologians. They were the unlettered *campesinos* who flocked into his office from all over the country seeking his understanding and support. Romero received them all and was always ready to listen, however much other important business was pending.

Though in many ways traditional in his piety and theology, Romero did not hesitate to speak out strongly in favor of the oppressed and condemn the injustices and corruption all too evident in an El Salvador dominated by a handful of wealthy families who rigged elections and organized military coups at will. His weekly sermons in the cathedral, broadcast to the nation over the archdiocesan radio station, catalogued human rights abuses and became the voice of those who had no voice. He followed to the letter the option for the poor made by the Conference of Latin American Bishops (CELAM) at Puebla that he himself attended in 1979.

In this he must be counted as belonging to a small band, suspected by Rome and deliberately sidelined by the group that came to dominate CELAM in the years after Puebla. He shared this distinction with others such as Samuel Ruiz of Chiapas, Lorscheider, Arns and Helder Câmara of Brazil, and Leónidas Proaño of Riobamba. In that age of national security states and military dictatorships, the professed aim of the conservative wing in the church, backed by Rome, was to eradicate liberation theology and suspected Marxist tendencies.

Romero was only too well aware of the price to be paid and rejoiced that the church was persecuted, along with himself, because of its stand for the poor, a sign of its authenticity. His courageous faith was supported by deep prayer and a reliance on God's continual guidance and presence. Often during meetings when some difficult problem was under discussion, he would slip out to present the case to the Lord and be found later on his knees in the chapel. And it was also on his knees that, after wide consultation, he prepared his homilies in the presence of God during the small hours of the morning. For, as he once told a journalist who asked where he found inspiration: "If it were not for this prayer and reflection with which I try to keep united to God, I would be no more than what St. Paul says: a clanging cymbal."

Romero was very much a saint for our times. He was not afraid to confront some of the major problems facing today's world: the widening gap between wealthy and poor both within and between countries, the corruption and impunity of the powerful, the exclusion of the marginalized from the benefits of society, violence caused fundamentally by social injustice, the absolute value attributed to wealth, private property, and national security. These problems are still with us, often in aggravated forms. What Romero had to say about how a Christian should react to them is therefore still highly relevant. He does not mince his words.

The following are excerpts from an article by Romero:

> A Christian who defends unjust situations is no longer a Christian....The wealthy person who kneels before his money, even though he goes to Mass, is an idolater and not a Christian....It is a caricature of love when alms-giving or an appearance of benevolence are used to cover over an absence of social justice....It is inconceivable to call oneself a Christian without making, like Christ, a preferential option for the poor.

□

Michael Campbell-Johnston, a Jesuit priest of the British Province, is pastor of a poor urban parish in El Salvador.

Thomas Merton
(1915–1968)

by Lawrence Cunningham

In a 1949 journal entry Thomas Merton wrote that if he was to become a saint, "I have not only to be a monk, which is what all monks must do to become saints, but I must also put down on paper what I have become." Those words were penned a year after the publication of *The Seven Storey Mountain*, a spiritual autobiography that, in its first year, sold over 600,000 copies, making Merton everywhere, except in his own monastery in rural Kentucky, a celebrity author.

Merton's early love affair with traditional monastic life is reflected also in *The Sign of Jonas*—a monasticism characterized by the round of daily prayer, work, silence, and biblical meditation. All this took quite a new turn when, as he famously described it in his book *Conjectures of a Guilty Bystander*, he was in downtown Louisville and realized, with the force of an epiphany, that he loved and identified with all the people going about their business and, further, that he and all monks were in community with them. "It was," he wrote, "like waking from a dream of separateness, of spurious self-isolation in a special world, the world of renunciation and supposed holiness. The whole illusion of a separate holy existence is a dream.... To think that for sixteen or seventeen years I have been taking seriously this pure illusion that is implicit in so much of our monastic thinking."

He went on: "I have the immense joy of being *man*, a member of a race in which God himself became incarnate....If only everybody could realize this! But it cannot be explained. There is no way of telling people that they are all walking around shining like the sun." If we could all see ourselves as we really are, he reflected, "there would be no more war, no more hatred, no more cruelty, no more greed...."

That intuition of solidarity more than justified Merton's plan to form networks of friendship with persons who were authentic searchers for truth and justice. From his adamantine conviction that precisely as a contemplative monk he could contribute to that search comes his vast exchange of letters with Latin American poets and intellectuals, peace activists, as well as a wide range of Protestant, Jewish, Muslim, and Buddhist writers. In the last decade of his life his study of Asian religions intensified, culminating in his fateful journey to Asia where he met his death by accidental electrocution on 10 December 1968—the same day Karl Barth died in Basel, Switzerland.

What explains the power of this monk who has now been dead for many years?

First, Merton was very much a modern searcher. Born in 1915 to an expatriate New Zealand–born father and an American mother of Quaker background, he led a vagabond life. His youthful zest for jazz and leftist politics, as well as his engagement with the modernist literary canon, bathed him in the acids of modernity. Like others of his generation, he had to find a substitute for the god(s) that failed. His monastic journals reveal a person who could be petty, angry, and, in a famous episode, ready to leave the monastery after an infatuation with a young nurse decades his junior. Readers soon learn that he was no plaster saint.

Secondly, while Merton himself recognized that a considerable part of his writing was not good, his best writing rings with religious authenticity. He brought to life for generations of ordinary people the vocabulary of monastic spirituality, the language of presence, compassion, purity of heart, solitude, and love in a new and fresh fashion. His finest work is not "pious." One finds in his informal conferences, in his essays and journal entries, lapidary observations, rooted in his own experience of prayer, about the reality of God in life. Here is Merton speaking to young monks:

> Life is very simple: we are living in a world that is absolutely transparent to God and God is shining through it all the time. This is not a fable or a nice story. It is true. God manifests himself everywhere, in every thing, in

people and in things and in nature and in events. You cannot be without God. It's impossible. Simply impossible.

He possessed a genuine poetic gift (his collected poems run to nearly nine hundred pages), with a capacity for the correct word. In *New Seeds of Contemplation*, for instance, avoiding the technical language of the theologians, he speaks of contemplation as "spiritual wonder" and "awakening" and "intuitive grasp" and "pure and virginal knowledge" and "spiritual vision" and as the "profound depth of faith." In the same book, he warns that this contemplative vision comes only to those who have compassion for others. Merton's own life, in his view, was an unfinished work. He never froze his monastic vision into some neo-Romantic vision of what a monk should be. His search was a monastic one, but every perceptive reader recognizes the profound authenticity of his self-discovery in the light of God's reality. He was an explorer of the Spirit.

□

Lawrence Cunningham is professor of theology at the University of Notre Dame. He has edited Thomas Merton: Spiritual Master: The Essential Writings *and is the author of* Thomas Merton and the Monastic Vision.

Martin Luther King, Jr.
(1929–1968)

by Leslie Griffiths and Wesley Williams

Martin Luther King, Jr., had all the intensity of an Old Testament prophet. When he announced "I have a dream" to the 250,000 people gathered at the Lincoln Memorial in August 1963, he might just as well have declared, "Thus saith the Lord." It was a word of judgment that, for all its severity, resonated with a note of hope. The crowd gave him its passionate backing. King's dream, of course, was a day when all the peoples of America, black and white, would know their true equality as the children of God. He rooted this vision deeply within the American dream itself, invoking the American constitution and also the national anthem to reinforce his point. "We hold these truths to be self-evident," he intoned, "that all men are created equal." But it was with words from a Negro spiritual that he brought his brilliant oration to its climax. "Free at last, free at last," he declared and thousands completed the sentence with him, "Thank God Almighty, we're free at last."

Martin Luther King, Jr., was born in 1929 into a Baptist family in the deep South. He completed his studies with a doctorate at Boston University before pastoring a church in Atlanta. He was soon called to head the Southern Christian Leadership Conference and spared no energy in fighting the deeply entrenched segregationism that was rampant at that time. He had learned from Mahatma Gandhi the method of nonviolent resistance and he developed it to a fine art.

Nonviolence to his mind was far from a passive response to social evil. As he wrote in his classic letter from Birmingham jail, "...it seeks to create such a crisis and foster such a tension that a community which has constantly refused to negotiate is forced to confront the issue." And through a series of well-publicized confrontations in cities throughout the South, King was able to change the mood of the American public and get equal rights on the statute book. Between 1957 and 1965, measures to provide nonsegregated schooling, equal housing, and full voting rights became law. King suffered imprisonment many times and he faced down a series of racist dinosaurs like Mayor Bull Connor of Birmingham and Governor George Wallace of Alabama. Behind them lurked the inchoate forces of the Ku Klux Klan.

King was anxious to challenge some of the conventional theological underpinnings of segregation. He rebutted the idea, put abroad by many fundamentalist preachers on the basis of Genesis

9:25–26, that blacks had been cursed forever and were destined to live out their lives as slaves. He reminded his listeners that since the beginning Christians had regularly disturbed the power structures of the towns and cities they visited. They were constantly accused of being "disturbers of the peace" and "outside agitators." But they went on in the conviction that they were a "colony of heaven" whose task it was to obey God rather than man. When the church is true to its nature, King argued, it always says, "Whosoever will, may come." And a recognition grows out of this, he concluded, "that all men are brothers because they are children of a common father."

And he also challenged the political inertia and lack of imagination that, in his view, had colluded with segregation for so long. He chided a succession of presidents from Eisenhower to Johnson for their unreadiness to give any kind of priority to the civil rights agenda. He was constantly pursued by the paranoid forces of the FBI under its leader J. Edgar Hoover, who were pledged to "get him." It was a truly remarkable achievement that, despite such obstacles, this Baptist preacher could spearhead a movement that yielded such conclusive results in the social, theological, and political fields, changing a whole culture. It was hardly a surprise when he was awarded the Nobel Prize for Peace in 1964.

For all his brilliance, King had feet of clay. Nowhere was his shadow side more evident than in his personal relationships. For all that, his wife, Coretta, and his children remained a tower of strength. More difficult for King was the way his commitment to nonviolence, which peaked with the Washington march and the

Civil Rights Act of 1964, began to give way to the more militant methods of Malcolm X and Stokely Carmichael. Yet the fruits of his labors can scarcely be denied.

Martin Luther King had seen a number of his close collaborators killed in the course of the struggle. The lowest point came in September 1963 when four little girls were killed in a bomb blast in the Birmingham church they attended. He had long understood that his own life was under daily threat and that it was only a matter of time before he too would be sacrificed. He was reconciled to that. "But it doesn't matter now," he told an enraptured audience, "I've been to the mountain top. I've looked over and I've seen the promised land. I'm not fearing any man. Mine eyes have seen the glory of the coming of the Lord." That was on 3 April 1968. He was assassinated the following day.

□

Leslie Griffiths is minister of Wesley's Chapel in London. Wesley Williams is executive director of the United Methodist Urban Services based in Boston, Massachusetts.

Pope John Paul II
(1920–)

---

by George Weigel

Speaking of some reporting that had stressed his accomplishments as a statesman, Pope John Paul II once said to me, a little whimsically, "They try to understand me from the outside. But I can only be understood from the inside." "Inside," Karol Wojtyla is a soul with a strikingly rich spiritual texture.

Wojtyla's is a Polish soul, not just geographically or ethnically, but in the sense of a soul formed by a distinctive history. As a boy, Karol Wojtyla learned the great lesson of modern Polish history: that the Polish nation survived through its culture when the Polish state was erased from the map for 123 years. Thus Wojtyla's soul reflects the truths that culture is the most dynamic element in history and that at the heart of culture is "cult": what we

---

honor, cherish, and worship. In Wojtyla's Polish soul, there formed, early on, the bedrock conviction that the Gospel remains the most compelling, history-transforming proposal in the world. The church has no need to be on the defensive, even in modernity; the church proposes, as he wrote in his encyclical letter of 1990, *Redemptoris Missio,* calmly and yet relentlessly.

The pope's is a Carmelite soul. Young Karol Wojtyla seriously considered a Carmelite vocation dedicated to contemplation. His life took a different direction, but the impress of his youthful reading in John of the Cross and Teresa of Avila has remained, in the conviction that the great truth of history is to be found on the cross, in Jesus abandoning himself to the will of the Father and being vindicated in that self-emptying by the resurrection. That, Wojtyla is convinced, is not one option in a global supermarket of "spiritualities"; that is the truth of the world.

The pope's Marian soul is both obvious and frequently misunderstood. In his vocational memoir, *Gift and Mystery,* John Paul II wrote that, on entering the Jagiellonian University in 1938, he thought he ought to put aside the conventional Marian piety of his youth to concentrate his spiritual life more directly on Christ. Shortly afterward, however, Jan Tyranowski, the lay mystic-tailor who first introduced Wojtyla to the Carmelite tradition, lent him the works of the seventeenth-century French theologian, Louis de Montfort. There, Wojtyla learned that "true devotion to Mary" (the title of Montfort's central work) pointed the Christian directly into the two great mysteries of Christian faith: the incarnation and the Trinity. Mary's last recorded words, at the wedding feast of Cana, were, "Do whatever he tells you." True devotion to Mary always points beyond Our Lady to her Son, the incarnate Word of God, and, through him, into the interior life of God, a Trinity of self-giving love and receptivity. Thus Mary is the paradigm of all discipleship. The church, including the Petrine church of office and authority, John Paul told the Roman Curia in 1987, takes its most fundamental form from a woman, Mary, and her self-surrendering fiat to the will of God.

John Paul's is also a dramatic soul. His early training for the theatre not only gave him useful skills, but a view of the human condition. The basic structure of our individual lives is dramatic, the pope believes: We all live in the gap between the "person I am" and the "person I ought to be." Moreover, those personal dramas "play" within a cosmic drama that has a divine scriptwriter, director, and, indeed, protagonist—for God himself entered the drama in order to redirect the story back toward its true destiny. This dramatic dimension of the pope's soul could allow him to say, precisely one year after he was shot down in St. Peter's Square, "In the designs of Providence there are no mere coincidences." The world is neither random nor purposeless; everything that happens is happening for a reason.

This most priestly of priests has something of a lay soul, in that he was formed into his priesthood by an intense set of friendships with the laypeople he served as a university chaplain in the early 1950s. As he shaped their young Christian lives, they shaped his experience of the priesthood and gave him, a decade before the Second Vatican Council, a profound insight into the universal call to holiness and the lay mission to sanctify the world. John Paul II's apostolic soul is formed by the conviction that the greatest service the church can do the world is to tell the world its true story: the story whose chapter headings are "Creation," "Fall," "Promise," "Prophecy," "Incarnation," "Redemption," "Sanctification," "the Kingdom." Telling that story also satisfies the longings of the pope's humanistic soul, which is shaped by his concern that the crisis of our times is the crisis in the idea of the human person. Christian humanism, he is convinced, is the answer to modernity's longing for a freedom tethered to truth and lived in goodness.

In the soul of John Paul II, Jesus Christ is the answer to the question that is every human life.

❏

George Weigel is the author of Witness to Hope: The Biography of Pope John Paul II.